D0618201

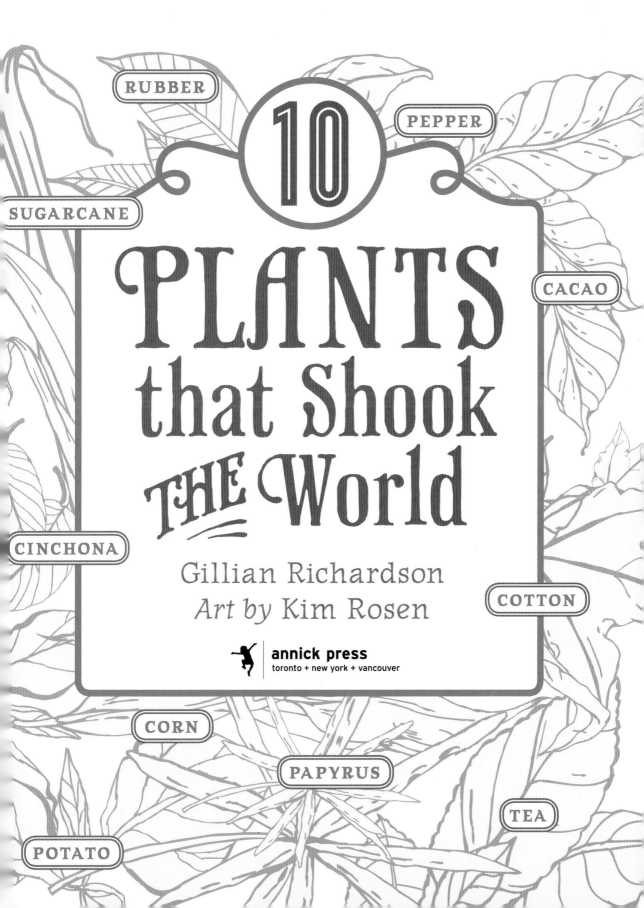

RUBBER

PEPPER

SUGARCANE

10

CACAO

PLANTS
that Shook
THE World

CINCHONA

COTTON

Gillian Richardson
Art by Kim Rosen

annick press
toronto + new york + vancouver

CORN

PAPYRUS

TEA

POTATO

Edited by Catherine Marjoribanks
Proofread by Tanya Trafford
Designed by Natalie Olsen/Kisscut Design

Annick Press Ltd.

We acknowledge the support of the Canada Council for the Arts, the Ontario
Arts Council, and the Government of Canada through the Canada Book Fund
(CBF) for our publishing activities.

ONTARIO ARTS COUNCIL
CONSEIL DES ARTS DE L'ONTARIO

Cataloging in Publication

Richardson, Gillian
10 plants that shook the world / Gillian Richardson ; art by Kim Rosen.

Includes bibliographical references and index.
Issued also in an electronic format.
ISBN 978-1-55451-445-8 (bound).—ISBN 978-1-55451-444-1 (pbk.)

1. Plants and history—Juvenile literature.   I. Rosen, Kim
II. Title.   III. Title: Ten plants that shook the world.

SB71.R53 2013   j581.6'3   C2012-905888-2

Distributed in Canada by: Published in the U.S.A. by Annick Press (U.S.) Ltd.
Firefly Books Ltd.   Distributed in the U.S.A. by:
66 Leek Crescent   Firefly Books (U.S.) Inc.
Richmond Hill, ON   P.O. Box 1338 Ellicott Station
L4B 1H1   Buffalo, NY 14205

Printed in China

Visit us at: www.annickpress.com
Visit Kim Rosen at: www.kimrosen.com
Visit Gillian Richardson at: www.books4kids.ca

For my sister, Joyce, the closest leaf on my family tree—G.R.

To Cara for her endless support—K.R.

CONTENTS

Introduction

Plants might start out as leafy things growing in the earth, but they can come into our lives in strange and unexpected ways. And some plants have even played an exciting role in our world's history.

You might think about plants when you're eating fruits and vegetables, but what about the pepper you add to your food, your cotton jeans, a sweet chocolate bar, or your movie-theater popcorn? All of these started life with roots and leaves.

Plant products like chocolate and cotton are part of our everyday lives, but it wasn't always that way. Can you imagine, for instance, a time when no one had even heard of rubber? Without it, how would our bike or car tires be possible?

Before the age of global exploration began in the 1400s, only indigenous peoples in remote places grew, harvested, and used many of the plants we depend on today. Then explorers began traveling between Europe, Asia, Africa, and the Americas. They found new plants and their products around the world. Some countries wanted to control the trading business when these new discoveries turned out to be incredibly popular—and profitable. (Wouldn't you like to have been the person to first bring chocolate to North America?) So then the race was on to control who grew these plants, who sold them, and who got the profits!

By the end of the 1800s, the movement of plants and people around the world had transformed it in unimagined ways. Plants like **tea**, **sugarcane**, **corn**, **potatoes**, **cacao**, and **pepper** became big business, and the race for profits often became more important than the lives of the people who grew them. Plant products like **cotton** and **rubber** improved the livelihoods of some, but caused unthinkable suffering for others. The bark of the **cinchona** tree gave the world a drug called quinine, saving countless lives from malaria, a disease that had held back exploration of tropical lands. And a rather ordinary-looking grass called **papyrus** became the first effective tool for sharing knowledge through writing.

These 10 plants are the source of profound changes, both good and bad, in the world. We use them with little thought to where they came from, or whose lives they might have affected on their journey through history. What you're about to discover is that without these plants, our lives today would be vastly different.

PAPYRUS

NAME

From the Greek *papuros*. Papyrus (pronounced *pa-PIE-rus*) is the name of both a plant and the paper made from it.

PROS + CONS

For the ancient Egyptians, papyrus was easy to make into paper at a low cost. It was thin, light, and easy to carry, and it could even be folded. It was strong enough to write on, although its surface was not as smooth as today's paper. It could be preserved, dry, for a long time. The downside? If it got wet, mold would grow and it would fall apart—just like modern paper.

BORN

In Egypt's Nile River delta. Now grows in swamps and shallow lakes throughout Africa, Madagascar, and Mediterranean countries, but is no longer found in its original home.

DISLIKES

Winter, when it does not grow.

LIKES

Full sun, and enough moisture to keep its roots wet all summer.

AGE

About 6,000 years old, as old as the first cities in Egypt. The oldest known piece of papyrus paper is an account sheet from some time around 2600 BCE.

STATS

Belongs to the sedge family of grassy plants. It grows in marshy areas, and has clumps of triangular green stems—which can stand as tall as a giraffe—topped by thin, feathery stalks. Papyrus is now mostly used as a decorative plant—it has greenish-brown flowers in summer and it produces nutlike fruits.

OSLO [2013]

Erika stares at the huge reed boat, Ra II, on display in the Kon-Tiki Museum. She can barely believe someone sailed all the way across the Atlantic Ocean in a craft made only from papyrus reeds. Wasn't that the same stuff the ancient Egyptians used to make paper? She made paper boats once for her little brother to sail in the park pond, but they soon got soggy and sank. Didn't the Egyptians worry about their boats falling apart right under them?

Looking closer, Erika can see how the bundles of reeds are tied tightly together, with thicker ones placed on the outside. So that's what kept the water from soaking right through to the middle! And the bow and stern are pulled up, probably to stop waves from washing over the boat. This boat has oars, but also a huge square sail made from a kind of cloth that started as papyrus, too.

If she closes her eyes, Erika can imagine herself back in ancient Egypt. She's in the bow of a small fishing boat, tending to the nets, while the fisherman sits in the stern and paddles. It's early morning, but the sun is already scorching, and she dips her hand into the cool Nile water.

Or maybe her reed boat is carrying an Egyptian scribe who has an important message to deliver to a government official . . . and it's written on papyrus paper, of course. No way they could have loaded these boats with the heavy stone tablets people wrote on before papyrus came along!

PLANT FACT

It appears the ancient Egyptians practiced recycling: they wrapped their mummies in layers of discarded papyrus.

The Story of Papyrus

THINK OF ALL THE WAYS PAPER TURNS UP IN YOUR EVERYDAY LIFE: the birthday card you gave your best friend, the novel you couldn't put down, that glossy paper for your art project, or the story you handed in for homework. But wasn't the invention of computers and email supposed to reduce our paper use? It sure hasn't turned out that way. Paper production is a huge industry, and it's expected to keep growing as the world population keeps rising. More and more people will be reading, writing on, and buying things made with paper. It's amazing to think that it all began with a plant, papyrus. Turning papyrus into paper was a discovery that launched the priceless tradition of recording the details of human history.

The book you are holding in your hands exists because of three inventions: the alphabet, writing, and—most important—paper, once made from papyrus.

HOW PAPYRUS PAPER IS MADE

It's hard to believe that among thousands of scraps of ancient papyrus, no evidence was found explaining how to make the paper. In the 1960s, an Egyptian scientist spent three years working to rediscover the process. First, he had to harvest the papyrus stem by cutting it close to the base. Then he peeled away the outer layer and cut the yellowish-white core into strips of equal thickness and length. After soaking them in water, he laid the strips side by side in two layers, one lengthwise and one crosswise. Next, the sheet was pounded to break down the fibers and release the natural glue that holds the layers together. Finally, the double-layered sheet was pressed until dry and smoothed with a stone. Voilà—writing paper!

THE VOYAGE OF THE Ra II

You can make a boat out of just about any material that will float—but how far will it take you? Experts used to believe that the boats made out of papyrus that were used by ancient Egyptians were strong enough to travel up and down the Nile, but too flimsy to survive an ocean crossing. That would have been impossible, they said, until wooden ships were built.

Then along came a Norwegian adventurer named Thor Heyerdahl, who decided to prove them wrong. In 1970, after experimenting with different kinds of boats, he and his crew sailed a craft built from papyrus reeds, the *Ra II*, 6,100 kilometers (3,700 miles), from Morocco to Barbados. His success proved that ancient peoples could have traveled widely—and it goes to show that reed boats are more seaworthy than you might think.

How Do You Spell That?

As far back as 5,000 years ago, people in many countries began to develop writing as a way to communicate. The most important system was known as the Phoenician alphabet. The Phoenicians were sailors and traders from the eastern Mediterranean Sea area, and because they traveled far and wide their alphabet was soon adopted by other cultures, including the Greeks and Romans. In fact, their alphabet was the forerunner of the 26-letter English alphabet we've used for centuries.

With an alphabet, writing became possible. But how could written information be preserved? Well, early people carved symbols and letters on wood or stone, or on clay tablets, using a pointed tool. Hardly a practical way to record details— imagine turning the pages when the book's made of stone! Then, about 3000 BCE, the Egyptians figured out how to make papyrus (from which we get the word "paper") from an ordinary marsh plant. For another 3,000 years, it was the best writing material available. How did this plant open up the world of communication, and help us understand what life was like in ancient times?

A very versatile plant!

Papyrus paper gives a special, lasting quality to painted colors and ink. That's why artists still enjoy using it to show images of Egyptian pharaohs and pyramids. In Egyptian art, you might also see a cluster of papyrus plants used to represent the marsh from which all life was thought to come—and hence life itself.

Papyrus fiber was woven as rope and used as a fabric for blankets, boat sails, baskets, mats, and sandals. The tough root was used to create bowls. It could be burned as fuel or dried to use as medicine. The cores of young plants could be cooked and eaten. And its sticky juice made it chewy; could it have been the first chewing gum, too? No wonder the Egyptians valued it so highly.

The Birth of the Book

Papyrus was used in single sheets, or several sheets were joined end to end to form a roll that could be up to 30 meters (100 feet) long, about the length of a basketball court. Normally, writing covered only one side. It was still not very easy to read a lot of text (unless you had a lot of room!), so the next format that came along was the **codex:** sheets were folded, stitched together, and protected with a cover. Now people could write on both sides of the paper and open it out flat to read it. That must have looked a lot like today's books.

Making Paper in 50 Easy Steps

So important was papyrus as a writing material that Egyptian rulers wouldn't let anyone take the "secret" of how to make it out of the country. Until the end of the seventh century, they did export the paper, but few examples of it have survived outside Egypt's dry desert climate. Archaeologists' discoveries of large amounts of papyrus in the garbage heaps of Egyptian towns show that it was a commonly used material up until the 10th century. That's when Arabs learned about a new paper that had been invented in China eight centuries earlier. It turned out to be easier and cheaper to create paper by mashing up various plant materials, such as hemp, bamboo, and tree bark. Pretty soon, papyrus was no longer as popular, and it gradually disappeared by the 11th century, the time of knights and crusades.

THE RHIND PAPYRUS

The ancient Egyptians were clever with numbers, too, and there's proof on papyrus. A scroll purchased in 1858 by A. Henry Rhind, a Scotsman fascinated by Egyptian culture, appears to be an early guide to mathematics. It may be a copy of an original document written around 1850 BCE. The problems, equations, and tables would have helped later civilizations learn more about math. The Rhind Papyrus is now part of the collection of the British Museum, in London.

The Past on Paper

People who study ancient papyrus documents—papyrologists—have learned that ordinary Egyptians used this early form of paper not only to write letters, but also to make lists and record details about their families and daily events in their lives. Many people living in Egypt spoke Greek, so we've learned how that language was used back then and how it has changed over time. Officials used papyrus for government documents, giving us an idea of how Egyptian society worked and what laws existed. Ancient literature and even music were recopied so they could be shared. Some texts found on papyrus do not exist in any other form, making these papyri a priceless record of ancient writings.

Many religious works, including the books of the Bible, were written on papyrus; among them are some of the oldest surviving biblical documents, known as the Dead Sea Scrolls. These documents were discovered in 1947 by shepherds exploring caves near the salt lake bordered by Jordan, Israel, and Palestine, and they have helped us understand the background of both the Jewish and Christian religions.

DEAD SEA SCROLLS

In 1778, a European visitor to Egypt bought a roll of papyrus documents from peasants. They turned out to be dated 191–192 CE! The visitor was probably horrified to watch the Egyptians burn many other rolls of these priceless historical documents just to enjoy the fragrant smoke! In the early 1800s, museums in Europe began to buy samples found in the ruins of ancient towns and burial sites. Thousands of sheets and scraps that had been discarded as garbage turned up in 1877. In all, an estimated 400,000 fragments of papyrus have been preserved and are being studied. Thankfully, enough pieces have survived to be our window into the ancient past.

TECHNOLOGY UNLOCKS THE SECRETS OF PAPYRUS

Papyrus scrolls unearthed from the remains of a scholar's library in Herculaneum, Italy, are finally giving up some of their secrets. Buried by the volcanic eruption of Mount Vesuvius in 79 CE, the scrolls were carbonized—burned by superhot lava—and squashed by rock into a solid mass. Little could be read of the black ink on blackened paper . . . until 2002, when scientists from Brigham Young University in Utah made a discovery. By adapting a technique developed by NASA to study the surface of planets from space, they were able to read the burnt papyrus manuscript fragments. They have been able to decipher historically significant writing that was considered lost to the eruption. A wealth of ancient records never seen before can now be preserved forever as digital files.

2

PEPPER

NAME
Pepper (black), comes from the Latin *piper (nigrum)*. Also known as "king of spices," "black gold."

PROS + CONS
The sharp, hot flavor of pepper stimulates stomach acids that help with digestion. But pepper has another, unexpected effect. It can make you sneeze. How? It irritates the nerve endings inside your nose...achoo!

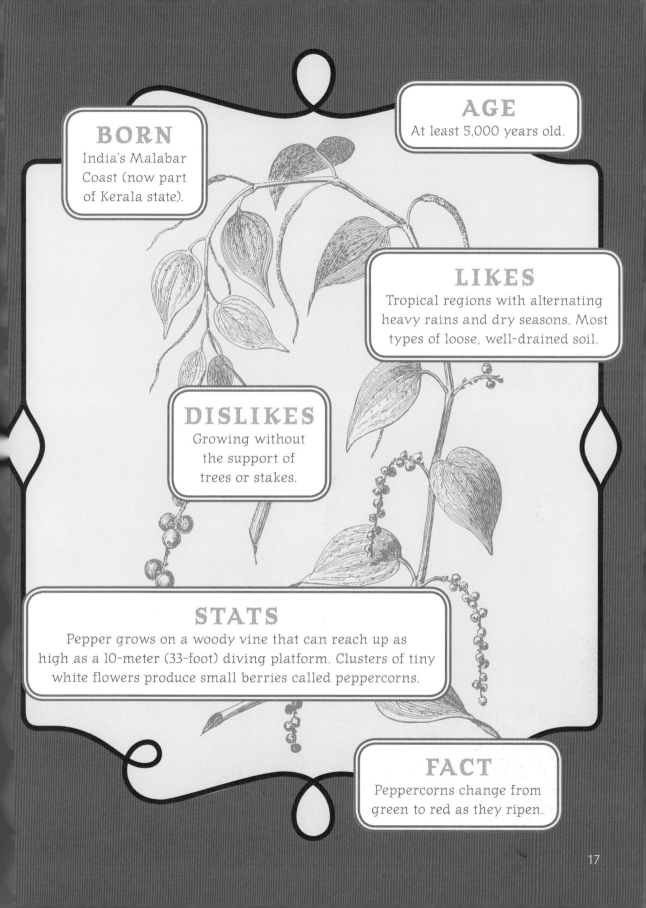

BORN
India's Malabar Coast (now part of Kerala state).

AGE
At least 5,000 years old.

LIKES
Tropical regions with alternating heavy rains and dry seasons. Most types of loose, well-drained soil.

DISLIKES
Growing without the support of trees or stakes.

STATS
Pepper grows on a woody vine that can reach up as high as a 10-meter (33-foot) diving platform. Clusters of tiny white flowers produce small berries called peppercorns.

FACT
Peppercorns change from green to red as they ripen.

THE SILK ROAD
[2,000 YEARS AGO]

The merchant trudges west over the endless desert beside the camel caravan. The hot sand burns through his sandals. He pulls a corner of his robe over his face to protect it from the searing winds. How can he keep a lookout for bandits when he can barely find the trail through the swirling clouds of sand? By nightfall, he knows, the caravan must reach the shelter of the fort with its precious cargo—not silk, bronze, or jade, but something worth stealing all the same. It is pepper. Black gold!

This is a dangerous road to travel with such valuable goods. So many terrors to face! There are thieves who strike without warning. And the land itself is an enemy. No animals or birds survive in this barren, bone-dry place. The camels plod on, poor beasts, thankfully born to deal with these dreadful conditions. It will be months before they reach the end of the trail, where there will be food, water, and safe shelter. It's a chance to rest before making the terrible trek home again to China.

Each night, the merchant can feel the presence of evil spirits. It's only the knowledge of how much wealth his cargo of pepper will bring that drives him onward.

PLANT FACT

The mummy of the Egyptian pharaoh Ramses II was found with his nostrils stuffed with peppercorns. Besides helping to preserve the body, this was seen as a way to honor the gods with a fragrance they'd like.

The Story of Pepper

OPEN A BOTTLE OF CINNAMON OR GINGER, and take a sniff. Does your mouth water? Do the tantalizing scents of these spices remind you of your favorite cookies and cakes? It seems like magic that just a pinch of spice will give such a distinct flavor to food.

For centuries, people have craved spices. These precious commodities were imported from the Far East, packed on camel caravans to travel overland, or loaded onto ships. Nomadic Arab traders sailed across the Indian Ocean taking spices through Egypt into Europe. Pepper—the world's most commonly used spice today—was one of the first items that China and India traded with Europe. Evidence of it has been found in artwork and writing in ancient Egyptian tombs.

It's amazing to think that the search for one treasured spice could result in discoveries of new lands. Even more astounding, countries went to war just to establish and control the major trade centers for pepper.

Pepper Is Hot in More Ways than One...

B Y THE FIRST CENTURY, rare black pepper had become a superstar, as highly prized as gold. Romans spent vast sums to buy it from India. And as the Roman Empire spread, so did pepper's mysterious power. It was used as medicine, as a sacred offering in religious rituals, and increasingly in food. It not only added flavor, it hid the bad taste of decay, making food still edible even if it wasn't all that fresh. As well, coating meat with peppercorns kept oxygen from reaching it, which slowed the process of spoiling. In the days before refrigerators, this helped to preserve the crucial food supply.

No wonder people wanted pepper. In fact, it was considered so valuable that they used it to pay their taxes and debts. And the story goes that in the fifth century, when the powerful city of Rome was overtaken by Visigoths, their leader, Alaric I, demanded thousands of pounds of peppercorns as part of a ransom to spare Roman lives.

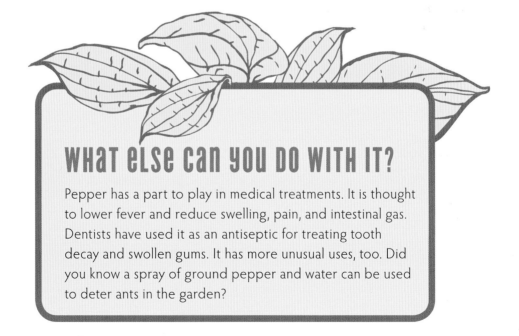

WHAT ELSE CAN YOU DO WITH IT?

Pepper has a part to play in medical treatments. It is thought to lower fever and reduce swelling, pain, and intestinal gas. Dentists have used it as an antiseptic for treating tooth decay and swollen gums. It has more unusual uses, too. Did you know a spray of ground pepper and water can be used to deter ants in the garden?

PAY WITH PEPPER

Imagine counting out peppercorns to pay for something
at the store! That's what people did in the Middle Ages.
In those days, coins contained different amounts of gold,
so their value was unreliable, but precious pepper made
a trustworthy currency. Payment with pepper might buy
a serf's freedom from a master. It was also an acceptable
way to pay rent, to provide a bride's dowry, to give as
a gift, and even to offer bribes to government officials.
One story tells of a sea merchant who wouldn't allow
dock workers to wear clothing with cuffs or pockets,
so they couldn't steal peppercorns from a ship's cargo.

Around the World for Pepper

THE ITALIAN EXPLORER MARCO POLO traveled to Asia in the 13th century and gathered all the information he could about the spice trade. When he came home, he helped to establish two Italian cities, Genoa and Venice, as Europe's centers for over-land spice shipments, with pepper at the top of the list. At one time, Europeans consumed over 2.7 million kilograms (6 million pounds) of pepper a year. You can imagine how rich that made the merchants selling pepper in Venice.

By the 1400s, other European countries were eager to get their share of that wealth. And they were tired of paying import duties imposed by traders bringing pepper by land. They knew where spices came from—the "Spice Islands" of the Far East. Could there be a better way to get there? By sea, perhaps? To find out, Spain sent Christopher Columbus west in his search, while the Portuguese explorer Vasco da Gama charted a route around the tip of Africa. Da Gama reached India in 1498, winning the race to the main pepper-growing region of Malabar. That victory gave Portugal control of both the pepper supply and the prices. Venice's monopoly on the market was broken . . . for a while.

THE OTHER PEPPER

Christopher Columbus failed to find the East Indies and the "Spice Islands" in 1492, so he brought home seeds from the Caribbean instead. He called one plant "pepper," but it was actually a chili pepper. Still, Europeans welcomed its spiciness as a substitute for black pepper. Chili peppers now grow everywhere and have even largely replaced black pepper in some countries. Part of the same plant species as colorful, sweet bell peppers, chilis are not even related to black pepper.

Once the sea route was open, Portugal couldn't keep other European countries from grabbing part of the pepper market. Soon, greed set off a tug-of-war for wealth and power. The Portuguese and Dutch fought for almost 200 years, until the Dutch East India Company eventually gained supremacy over the seas. By the 1700s, it was the world's richest trading organization, creating a secure supply of spices for European markets.

Hot, spicy pepper fueled much of this historic change. But once explorers found they could sail clear around the globe, spices were no longer so rare—and they certainly were no longer worth fighting wars over. Soon all kinds of spices were grown worldwide. But one thing didn't change: pepper is still king, and today it accounts for about a quarter of the world's spice trade.

PEPPER RICHES

When America's fast clipper ships made that country a world trader in the early 1800s, Salem, Massachusetts, became a prosperous shipping center. In fact, it supplied such a large part of the world's pepper that a Salem merchant, Elias Hasket Derby, became one of the first millionaires in America by importing it. And what did he do with his spicy wealth? He gave some of it to the prestigious Yale University, in Connecticut.

3

TEA

NAME
From the Chinese word *t'e*
(pronounced *tay*).

PROS + CONS
Tea can be either a relaxing break or an energizing pick-me-up. A cold tea bag can be used to take the itch out of insect bites, cool a sunburn, or soothe puffy eyes. There is some scientific evidence to suggest that tea may prevent certain diseases, including cancer, because it contains antioxidants. What's the downside? The caffeine in tea can act as a diuretic—so tea drinkers might make more trips to the bathroom.

AGE

Nearly 5,000 years old. Some say that the Chinese emperor Shen Nung discovered tea by accident in 2737 BCE. He was drinking hot water when the dry leaves of a tea plant fell into his cup—and he liked it! Is it true? It's certainly a good story.

BORN

China.

LIKES

Moist, well-drained soil, partly shaded. Warm temperatures.

DISLIKES

Very cold weather, below -18°C (0°F). Fungus, and insects that chew its leaves.

STATS

Tea comes from an evergreen shrub with shiny, pointed leaves and fragrant white flowers. Wild tea plants can grow nearly as tall as a two-story house, but they are pruned to about the height of a doorknob to encourage new growth.

BOSTON [1773]

Edward feels a little silly, dressed up like an Indian with coal dust "warpaint" on his face, and carrying a hatchet—which his commander insists on calling a "tomahawk." But he knows the men haven't gathered in Boston's harbor for a silly reason. Edward and about 200 of his fellow colonists have decided to demonstrate their refusal to submit to unfair English taxation of Americans by boarding three ships bringing tea, and dumping the cargo into the water.

On the hill overlooking the harbor, Edward shuffles his feet nervously. He's glad when the signal comes to march to the wharf and onto the ships. The men begin whooping war cries, and soon they are swinging their hatchets to break open the tea chests and heave them overboard.

They watch the tea floating among the armed British ships that sit nearby. No one attempts to stop them, even though it takes several hours to complete the destruction. All the while, Edward worries where this act of rebellion might lead.

PLANT FACT

In a famous Australian song, "Waltzing Matilda," the "jolly swagman" watched and "waited while his billy boiled" over a campfire. He was making himself a cup of tea!

The Story of Tea

Would you like a cup of tea? Will that be orange pekoe, Earl Grey, or Darjeeling? Green, white with peach, lemon, or black currant? Hot or iced? It's hard to know what to choose among so many kinds and flavors of tea. Nowadays, people all over the world (mostly adults) drink it with meals or for a refreshing break at any time. It's second only to water as the beverage people drink most often, so it's hard to believe it was once a rare and expensive treat.

If you went back almost 5,000 years, you would only have found tea growing on Chinese farms. Then, in the 13th century, Buddhist monks took it to Japan, where it became the focus of formal tea ceremonies still enjoyed today. Dutch and Portuguese traders in the 1600s knew a fortune could be made selling it to Europe. Tea quickly became all the rage in England, even though how it grew remained a mystery for almost another 200 years. Who would have thought a plant like tea could change the social and cultural habits of people everywhere, inspire entire new industries, and even become mixed up in a war?

DID TEa START a WaR?

A tea party on a sailing ship? In the middle of the night?

In the late 1700s, America was still a British colony. England was trying to raise money to cover the costs of wars it had been fighting for years against other European countries. So, if American colonists wanted to buy things like paper, glass, lead, and tea—things they could only buy from English traders—they were expected to pay a big tax to the English. And worse still, they had no say in what England did with the money. Refusal to pay the tax was one way for the Americans to show their resentment.

Things came to a head in Boston Harbor on December 16, 1773. When three ships carrying tea arrived from England, a group of colonists called the Sons of Liberty refused to let them unload the cargo. They ordered the ships to leave. But that was against the law unless their cargo was unloaded...or a tax paid. No way! About 200 men boarded the ships and tossed 342 tea chests overboard. England then closed Boston Harbor, and America's rising anger was unstoppable. The War of Independence was soon underway, ignited in large part by the "Boston Tea Party."

Trading for Tea

Tea came to Europe at a time when water was unsafe to drink without boiling. The alternative, ale—a kind of beer—was not a good thirst-quencher for kids, or for anyone trying to get a day's work done. How convenient to have a tasty, non-alcoholic drink like tea that only required hot water! By the early 1800s, the English consumed an astonishing 9 million cups of tea a year.

China was still the only source of tea, and the Chinese demanded payment in silver. But England didn't have much silver. How could the East India Company, which imported the tea to England, find enough silver to buy all the tea needed to meet the demand? Well, another plant was the answer—the opium poppy grown in India.

Opium is a dangerous narcotic, which means it is a highly addictive drug. Even though it was banned in China in 1729, some merchants were still willing to buy smuggled opium. And they were prepared to pay for it with silver—just what England needed.

As long as England could trade Indian opium to China for silver, it could use that silver to buy tea. But in 1840, China decided to stop the illegal opium trade and faced off with England in what were called the Opium Wars. When the dust settled, England had gained possession of Hong Kong, and China had opened more of its ports.

England could see its days were numbered as the only dealer of opium. If the opium–silver exchange dried up, how would England buy tea? Now America got in on the act too, using its faster clipper ships to challenge England's hold on the tea trade.

How Tea Leaves Become Tea

MACHINES MIGHT DAMAGE THE TENDER PLANTS, so to process tea, skilled pickers pluck just the top two leaves and the final bud from the tea plant. Women usually do this task because of their smaller fingers. The collected leaves are then spread out in the sun in thin layers on trays or fabric until they go limp (called **withering**). Next, the leaves are rolled and crushed to release any remaining moisture.

Spread out again in a warm place, the leaves are allowed to ferment for two to four hours. That's when chemical reactions with oxygen in the tea leaves darken the color and intensify the flavor. At the right time, the leaves are heated to stop the fermentation process, and then the tea is quickly cooled, sorted by quality, and sealed in airtight packages or put into tea bags.

What's the difference between the types of tea? Black tea is fermented, and green tea isn't. A third type, oolong (from the Chinese *wu-long,* meaning "black dragon"), is only partly fermented.

IS IT REALLY TEA?

Maybe you've tasted herbal teas or seen adults drink them. There are lots, like cinnamon apple, peppermint, chamomile, and blueberry. Surprise...they aren't made from tea leaves. Herbal "tea" is made by taking the leaves, flowers, seeds, or roots of other plants and steeping them in boiling water. Flavored tea, though, does contain black or green tea leaves, along with another plant to produce a distinctive taste, such as vanilla or jasmine.

Tea Spy

ENGLAND NEEDED A NEW SOURCE OF TEA. Could it grow tea in its own colonies with a suitable climate, like India? Well, first it needed top-quality plants and seeds, and there was only one place to get them: China.

England sent a botanist, Robert Fortune, to secretly explore China's interior regions to obtain tea plants and seeds, and learn how to cultivate them. Fortune discovered that green and black tea came from the same plant species, something that hadn't been understood before. Now they knew the difference between varieties was a result of how the tea was processed.

With this stolen knowledge, England was able to establish tea plantations in Assam, India, by 1860. The new industry would boom in the late 1800s as India produced about 91 million kilograms (200 million pounds) of tea—enough for about 33 billion tea bags. Today it is grown in more than 40 countries—and 3.5 *billion* kilograms are produced annually. India tops the list for tea drinking.

More Than Just a Drink

ONCE TEA BECAME AN AFFORDABLE DRINK in Europe and America, it began to change the way people socialized. They gathered in tea houses to catch up on news and gossip. People looked forward to these midday "tea breaks" as an excuse for refreshment and conversation.

Tea also became another name for a social event, or a meal. The wealthier classes served "low tea"—small, friendly afternoon gatherings with elegant cakes around low tables—saving their big meal for evening. Working-class folks, on the other hand, adopted the idea of "high tea." That might sound like a fancy party, but it was actually a main meal of meat and vegetables served at a dining table in the late afternoon, when they finished work in the factories.

The tea ceremony is a centuries-old tradition that is still popular today. Everything is carefully prepared for this occasion by a well-trained tea master—the plants and flowers in the formal garden, the purifying water for guests to wash their hands and rinse their mouths, and the special tea dishes. Guests bend down to go through a low doorway into the tea room, in an expression of humility. Kneeling on straw mats, they eat a meal and share a bowl of green tea. The ceremony is heavily influenced by the Buddhist religion and its principles of harmony, respect, purity, and tranquility. After the tea ceremony is finished, guests leave refreshed in body and mind.

A New Pottery Industry

ONCE THE WORLD HAD A NEW DRINK, it needed something to brew it in and drink it from. So a new industry was born.

The Chinese had developed porcelain—a hard, shiny pottery made by firing clay at high temperatures, then decorating and glazing it—as early as the seventh century. They brewed tea in large bowls and drank it lukewarm from smaller bowls with no handles. Millions of pieces made their way to Europe as ballast to make tea-laden ships more stable. With the popularity of tea in England, businessmen saw an opportunity. Why couldn't England make its own "china" dishes to replace the traditionally used stoneware, which didn't stand up well to heat or to liquids?

Teapots with spouts for easy pouring and cups with handles, for hot tea, were a response to the new tea craze. Then people needed milk jugs and sugar bowls, spoons for stirring, saucers to hold the spoons, and plates for cakes and biscuits. Soon all these things were in mass production at England's factories. Josiah Spode and Josiah Wedgwood both manufactured fine china with classical designs and colors. The companies that bear their names still make china today.

4

SUGARCANE

NAME

From Sanskrit *sharkara* and Arabic *sukkar*. Also known as "white gold."

PROS + CONS

Did you know that sugar, besides being a sweetener, might help heal skin infections by preventing bacteria from growing? We also use it to preserve fruits (think of jam and marmalade). As a food, though, sugar is only good for its sweet taste and its calories. Unfortunately, it has none of the nutrients found in fruits or vegetables. Sugar is partly responsible for the billions spent on dental care and other health problems, like diabetes.

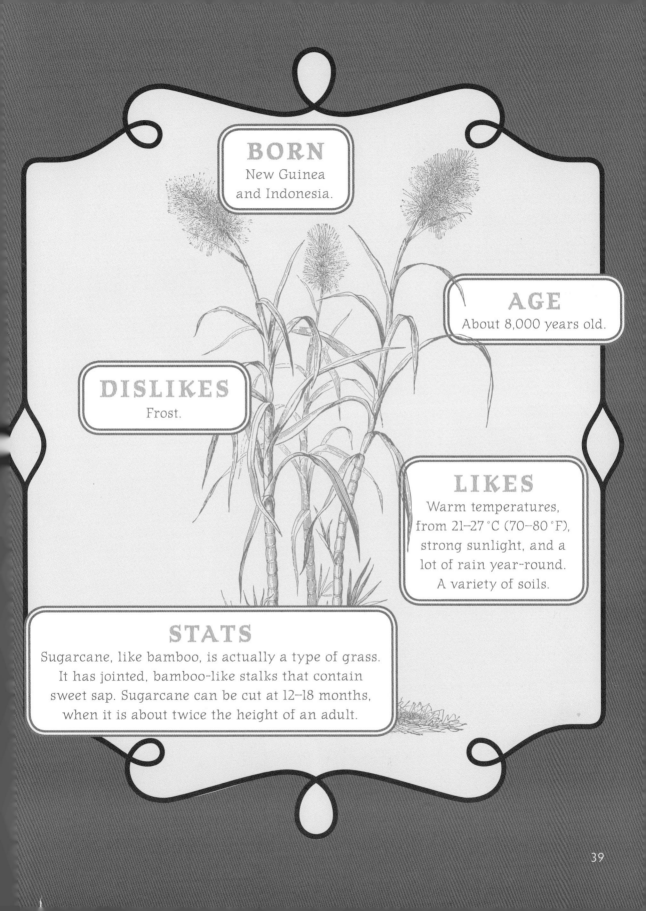

BORN
New Guinea
and Indonesia.

AGE
About 8,000 years old.

DISLIKES
Frost.

LIKES
Warm temperatures,
from 21–27 °C (70–80 °F),
strong sunlight, and a
lot of rain year-round.
A variety of soils.

STATS
Sugarcane, like bamboo, is actually a type of grass.
It has jointed, bamboo-like stalks that contain
sweet sap. Sugarcane can be cut at 12–18 months,
when it is about twice the height of an adult.

BARBADOS [1680]

The slave swings the machete blade at the sugarcane. Each time it strikes the base of a thick stalk, his muscles scream. Sweat runs down his aching back and arms, stinging the cuts on his hands. With each passing hour, it is harder to keep a tight grip on the tool. Best to find a rhythm; sing the old songs from his African homeland, in his head. Many hot days of back-breaking harvest remain on this sugar plantation.

Not that the work will end when harvest is done. When he isn't out here cutting in the field for 12 hours a day, he's sent to work in the mill, where it's even hotter. And no less dangerous. Out here he faces cuts if the machete slips, or from the sharp-edged cane leaves. Or bites from the poisonous snakes that lurk in the undergrowth. In the mill, he's already suffered burns from the super-hot steam, and he has been lucky so far to avoid breaking an arm in the rollers that crush the cane.

This cane crop will have to be processed right away. That means 18-hour shifts in the suffocating heat of the mill for some, all day or all night, with no slacking off. How could they, when they're watched over and threatened constantly by overseers with whips? No one cares if they're hungry, injured, or too tired to do the work. It seems as though there is no escape from the misery except in death.

PLANT FACT

Which sugar doesn't belong in this group: white, brown, icing, maple? They all come from plants, but only one of them comes from a tree. Maple sugar is made by boiling the water out of maple tree sap. The others are made from either sugarcane or sugar beets.

The Story of Sugar

Candy, cookies, soft drinks, and other sweet treats—it's hard to find any prepared food that doesn't contain sugar. What would Halloween or Valentine's Day be without candy? "Sweet" describes many things we like, and we use "sugar" or "sweetie" as expressions of affection. But there's another side to sugar's rise to stardom: its huge toll on human lives and health, and profound changes to the population makeup and environment in some parts of the world. Why has our favorite taste sensation caused so much turmoil?

The Taste that Changed the World...

THE FIRST SWEETENER, USED FOR THOUSANDS OF YEARS, WAS HONEY. Sugarcane was cultivated around 1000 BCE, and early travelers took it throughout the Far East. Alexander the Great may have been the first European to taste it, in 325 BCE. In the seventh century, Arab traders brought both sugarcane and the technology for processing it to Egypt.

Sugar became so popular with Europeans that in the late 1400s the Spanish and Portuguese decided to step up production. They put slaves from West Africa to work planting and harvesting the cane on several warm, humid islands off Africa's Atlantic coast. Still, more and more people in Europe craved sugar's sweet taste. Where could they grow more of it?

Christopher Columbus, off to find new trade routes to the east to secure access to spices, instead discovered the perfect growing climate for sugarcane in the West Indies. The Spanish quickly established the first plantations on Hispaniola (now Haiti and the Dominican Republic), while the Portuguese took sugarcane to Brazil.

A Dangerously Sweet Habit

In London in 1319, the price of sugar was equivalent to US$100 per kilogram (2.2 pounds). That's almost 100 times what you would pay now in the supermarket. By the late 1500s in England, tooth decay had become a growing problem—but only for the wealthy, who were the first people to eat sugar in large amounts. Queen Elizabeth I had such a "sweet tooth" that hers turned black with decay. When sugar prices finally dropped in the 1700s, tea with sugar quickly became part of the daily diet for everyone.

Local indigenous tribes were forced to work the plantations that spread from island to island. But many did not survive the strenuous hand-planting and harvesting, while others died from smallpox or scarlet fever brought by Europeans. West African slaves became the new workforce, since they knew about farming and were already used to a tropical climate. Starting in 1510, the tidal wave of human cargo delivered by slave ships to the sugar plantations—around 3 million people in total—would continue for about 300 years.

Other Europeans realized that vast profits could be made from sugar, and soon settlers were flocking to the "sugar islands" to make their fortunes. England, France, and Holland all established colonies in the Caribbean during the mid-1600s, sometimes fighting each other to control them. And the war for profit was waged at sea as well. There was no point in harvesting sugarcane if you couldn't export it and sell it, and England, with its superior naval power, prevented the other countries from carrying sugar overseas.

SWEET BEETS

Another source of sugar—beets—first gained attention during the War of 1812. France's enemy, England, blockaded shipping routes from the West Indies, cutting off the supply of cane sugar. To take its place, France's Emperor Napoleon established a sugar beet industry, and by the late 1800s, beets provided a third of Europe's sugar. Sugar beets—a white root vegetable with a high concentration of sucrose—are sliced and mixed with hot water to draw out their sweet juice, which is then refined into crystals, much like cane sugar. Sugar beets need four times the amount of land cane does, but they can be grown in cooler climates. And it's hard to tell the difference between beet sugar and cane sugar.

HOW Cane Becomes SUGaR...
and OTHER STUFF

At harvest time, sugarcane is cut close to ground level, where the sugar content is highest. Leaves are stripped off, or sometimes the cane field is burned to remove the leaves without damaging the sugar-rich stem. At the mill, crushing the stems releases juice. The juice is then boiled to a thick syrup (molasses) and dried into brown sugar crystals. Further refining creates the familiar white sugar crystals. Grinding white sugar to a fine powder creates icing sugar. Look at the labels on food packages for the term "sucrose," which is the chemical name for natural sugar.

The fibrous material left after crushing the canes—bagasse—can be dried and burned as fuel to run the sugar mill. Cane stalks also make a building material called fiberboard, while the leaves may become roofing shingles or cattle feed.

Sweet and Sour

Europe's demand for sugar rose from 10,000 tons in 1700 to 150,000 tons a century later, making it the main crop in the West Indies until the mid-1800s. On some islands, including Barbados, Jamaica, and Cuba, sugar became virtually the only crop, with devastating effects for the land.

Picture a small tropical island—lush vegetation, sustained by a balance of sun, rain, and balmy winds, home to indigenous peoples like the Caribs, and to wildlife such as monkeys and parrots. But to turn small farms into huge sugar plantations, Europeans in the 1600s cut down rainforests, destroying natural habitats and exposing the soil to erosion by salt-laden wind and heavy rains. Sugar growing used up the soil's nutrients, and most of the island's fresh water was diverted for irrigation, leaving little for people or animals. The parts of the sugarcane that weren't useful after harvest were burned, releasing pollution into the air.

Soon the islands were deforested, and the timber needed for fuel to process the cane had to be brought from America. The tropical paradise would never be the same again. Sadly, sugarcane cultivation is believed to have caused more environmental damage than any other crop. Now that we know this, less destructive growing practices are being considered, such as leaving cane "trash" on the fields as compost so fewer fertilizers will be needed.

FUEL UP ON SUGAR

The air in Brazil might have a sweet scent—or, at least, less automobile pollution. Over half of Brazil's abundant sugarcane harvest is used to produce ethanol, a by-product left after the juice from the cane has fermented. Ethanol, usually blended with gasoline, can be used as clean fuel for cars. In Brazil, 9 out of 10 new cars can burn ethanol. Studies are being done to find out if it works as efficiently as gasoline.

Free to Work

WHILE THE SUGAR INDUSTRY FLOURISHED from the 1700s to the mid-1800s, a shift was taking place in the population of the West Indies. Black slaves and people of mixed race soon vastly out-numbered Europeans. But opposition to slavery was growing in Britain, and it resulted, in 1834, in the Emancipation Act, which freed slaves in all British colonies. Other countries soon followed suit.

Freedom came with a price, though. Ex-slaves now had to compete for work with others, including "indentured" workers from India and Asia who had agreed to work for five years, after which they could go home if they wished. Many chose to stay. Their descendants, along with a large African population, are now part of the unique cultural mix in the West Indies. Each ethnic group has contributed its own customs, language, music, and food to the modern-day Caribbean region.

Today, sugar is grown in over 100 countries, with three-quarters of production coming from cane and the rest from beets. Europe, Brazil, and India are the main producers.

THE FUN SIDE OF SUGAR

The appeal of sugar created a whole new food culture. The 1904 World's Fair, in St. Louis, Missouri, helped to promote such sweet treats as soft drinks, ice cream cones, Jell-O, and cotton candy. While too much sugar can create health problems, the addition of sugar to many foods makes them more appetizing. For instance, when used in tomato-based products like spaghetti sauce, it boosts flavor. Back in 1915, the average person in the United States ate about 7 to 9 kilograms (15 to 20 pounds) of sugar each year. Today, it's estimated we eat at least our weight in sugar annually.

5

COTTON

NAME
From the Arabic *al-qutun*.
Also known as "King Cotton."

PROS + CONS

Cotton is recyclable. Your old denim jeans can even be reused to make insulation for buildings. But growing cotton in the first place is not so hot for the environment, because it requires more hazardous pesticides than any other agricultural crop. That means health risks for people and livestock, major die-offs of fish, birds, and beneficial insects, and contamination of surface and ground water. Organic cotton is catching on, though. It is grown without pesticides or fertilizers, uses beneficial insects to control pests, and needs less irrigation because organic matter in the soil holds moisture.

AGE

At least 7,000 years old—cotton was born when the last ice age ended.

BORN

In the world's tropical regions. Cotton was probably first cultivated by farmers in India, China, and Peru.

DISLIKES

Frost. And boll weevils, which chew on its unopened pods.

LIKES

Any climate or elevation, as long as it gets lots of rain in its first three months.

STATS

A shrubby plant with white flowers and pods called bolls, which contain seeds and hairy fibers. All parts of the cotton plant are useful in some way. Cottonseed oil is an ingredient in food products, and leftover seed hulls become cattle feed.

51

NEW ENGLAND [1836]

Beth trudges along the streets of her New England town and meets other mill girls headed for the cotton factory. She pulls her scarf tighter, but the morning chill isn't really what's on her mind today. In only a couple of weeks—just past her 18th birthday—she'll be finished this 10-month stretch at the spinning frames. Since the fall, she's faced 14-hour days doing this monotonous work—standing, constantly checking the cotton threads for snags or breaks, enduring the deafening noise of the machines, sweltering in the heat of the closed, lint-filled room. She'll be glad to go back home to help on the family farm for the summer.

She's happy, too, with the money she's earned in the factory. It means her brother can study for a good job. But school is not in the cards for Beth. She'll be back at the mill at the end of summer. Still, this job pays much better than the meager amount she'd earn as a servant or seamstress, the only other kinds of jobs she'd be allowed to do.

Up ahead, Beth spots her friends from the mill—Sarah, Honor, and Emma. She hurries to catch up. They've got their heads together—they're probably talking about the gathering that's been planned for that evening at a park in town. They've all heard rumors of pay cuts. Of course the mill owners always want to make more money, but no one is prepared to work for less. Beth doesn't know the woman who is supposed to speak at the gathering on their behalf. Some of the mill girls were surprised, others shocked, that a woman would stand up against the mill owners that way. Whatever happens, Beth hopes her job is safe. She knows how much her family is depending on her income.

PLANT FACT

Fire hoses were once made out of cotton lined with rubber. And the filament in Thomas Edison's very first light bulb was made of twisted cotton.

The Story of Cotton

THE WHOLE WORLD LOVES COMFORTABLE, EASY-TO-WEAR COTTON. It washes and dries faster than wool, and wrinkles less than linen (which is made from the flax plant). It is also much less expensive and more practical than silk. But cotton wasn't always inexpensive or easy to find. The first kinds of cotton fabrics brought to Europe by traders—muslin and calico—were rare and exotic. It was not until the mid-1700s that cotton really caught the world's attention. It triggered remarkable changes in the way goods were produced. The new technologies used to produce it gave rise to inhumane working conditions in factories and on slave-based plantations. And how on earth did cotton lead to one of the deadliest wars in history?

INVENTIONS SPARKED BY COTTON

John Kay invented a lever-operated **flying shuttle** that wove fabric much faster and wider than the old hand shuttle, which had to be passed back and forth through a loom by one person.

James Hargreaves created the **spinning jenny** to spin dozens of threads at once.

Richard Arkwright patented the **water frame**, which produced fine thread and was powered by water.

Samuel Crompton's **spinning mule** spun thousands of threads onto spindles for weaving.

James Watt's adaptation of a **steam engine** first powered machines in cotton mills.

Boom Time for Cotton

As EUROPE BECAME MORE INDUSTRIALIZED, cotton, brought in its raw form from colonial India, became one of Britain's main economic engines. Farm families in England could spin and weave about 225,000 kilograms (500,000 pounds) of cotton per year by hand, but by 1784, new and speedier machines in mills were turning out an astonishing 7 million kilograms (almost 16 million pounds) a year. The price of cotton for the consumer got a lot cheaper, and, not surprisingly, workers flocked to the new factory towns during the Industrial Revolution as the demand for cotton exploded.

In the United States, where some cotton had long been grown in the South, all it took was one invention to boost this small-scale practice into a major industry. In 1793, Eli Whitney's cotton gin made separating the cotton plant's fibers from its seeds, which had always been done by hand, a much easier, faster, machine-based job. Suddenly, cotton farmers could make vast profits from selling their raw cotton to cotton mills in England and America's northern states. Southern farmers rushed to plant more cotton.

THE COTTON GIN

Eli Whitney's simple device held cotton's sticky seeds in its wire teeth while rotating hooks pulled the fibers free. Where one worker might hand-clean only one-half to a full kilogram (1–2 pounds) of fibers a day, many cotton gins operating together could get through an incredible 225 kilograms (500 pounds). Cotton grew well in the southern United States, and this new invention soon made it so profitable that it became the number-one crop. Before the Civil War, the United States supplied two-thirds of the world's cotton output.

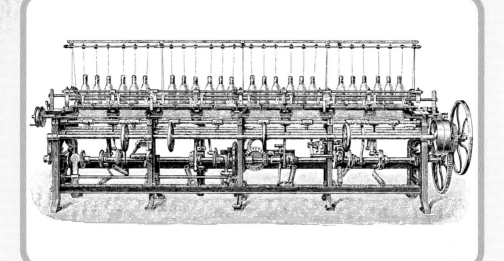

CHILD LABOR

In England's new "working class"—a category that didn't
exist until the Industrial Revolution brought people
to the cities to work—nine out of ten factory workers
were women or children, as young as six years old. From
overcrowded row houses, children in threadbare clothing
hurried through the streets at dawn. Smoky air from the
cotton mill burned their lungs. And there was no fresh
air to be found inside the massive buildings where they
worked for the next 12 to 14 hours. The roaring steam
engines that powered the weaving machines made it
almost too hot to bear. Worse was the constant fear:
children were made to crawl under the fast-moving looms
to tie loose threads together, and fingers or a sleeve
might easily be caught. Or a child could be dragged
into the spinning machines and killed as shuttles zoomed
back and forth and weaving frames snapped open and
shut. For facing all these risks, the children earned only
a few pennies a day. Child labor was a terrible outcome
of the "factory system," which aimed to keep the costs of
production low and profits high.

Forced Labor

To BOOST THE WORKFORCE on their plantations, Southern owners bought slaves who had previously worked tobacco, sugar, and rice crops. Slave ships brought still more workers from Africa, and they traveled to America in the most dreadful conditions. Packed in rows below deck, shoulder to shoulder, 500 to a ship, they were scarcely able to move for up to three months. Maggots crawled in open sores rubbed raw by the iron manacles that gripped their ankles and necks. There was no fresh air to relieve the suffocating heat or the overbearing stink of human waste that collected in the holds. For as many as 20 out of every 100 slaves, life ended on those ships.

For the survivors—almost 2 million slaves had arrived by 1850—endless toil and cruelty awaited them on cotton plantations. Daybreak found them already clearing land, planting, weeding, or picking sacks of cotton. They worked almost nonstop in the hot sun. Overseers expected at least 90 kilograms (200 pounds) per day from each picker. Mothers carried their babies with them, and even young children had to hoe cotton. Work quickly and the reward was . . . more work! Slow down, and feel the sting of the overseer's whip.

Workers who weren't picking cotton might work in the corn fields, or tend the farm animals, or chop wood for cooking fires. At day's end, the slaves returned to their crudely built shacks to cook a meal of corncakes or mend their ragged clothes. After a few hours' sleep on a dirt floor with only a thin blanket, the daily grind began again.

Stories of freedom in the north fueled slaves' dreams of escape. But was running away worth the risk? If captured, they were brutally beaten, maybe branded, or sold at slave auctions, never to see their families again.

ℋ Nation Divided

IN MOST SOUTHERN STATES, slavery was seen as essential to the agriculture-based economy that was growing rich on the 4 million bales of "King Cotton" produced every year. But things were different in the North. There, the economy was more industrial. In city factories, workers were free to sign on as employees. And as new states joined the American nation throughout the 1800s, they could chose to be either "free" or "slave" states.

Some Americans protested against slavery, calling it inhumane and demanding that it be abolished. When Abraham Lincoln became the 16th president of the United States, he supported these abolitionists, and his opposition to slavery resulted in the South

boldly choosing to leave the Union and become an independent nation. Before long, the deep divide between pro- and anti-slavery states led to the Civil War (1861–65), which pitted North against South in a deadly clash of economies, attitudes, and traditions.

As the war began, the North blockaded sea ports, cutting off the South's ability to sell its cotton. The South thought its best cotton customer, England, would come to its rescue. But England chose not to take sides. It had abolished slavery in 1834 throughout the British Empire. Instead, England simply began buying its cotton from India and Egypt. The South quickly found itself with few resources to keep up a long battle—except a lot of cotton no one would buy.

A War Lost

As the South had no well-developed road or rail system, and no industry to build wagons, the movement of both soldiers and food was agonizingly slow. To make matters worse, no mills supplied uniforms or tents, and no factories made boots, because the South had always depended on importing such basics from Europe or the North. Prepared or not, the soldiers took up arms against the North in a war that would forever change America.

Young Civil War soldiers faced seemingly endless marches, taking them farther than they'd ever been from home. Sometimes the mail caught up with them, bringing news of the family or a package of socks, warm pants, or boots to replace those worn out from rough roads. But more often the cold, relentless rain dogged them, and treks through waist-deep water in swamps left many sick and dying from fever and chills. At the end of the road, they might find sleep in a muddy field with no shelter, and another cold, dry meal of hardtack—a type of plain cracker—and salt pork.

Maybe the worst part for soldiers was leaving the bodies of their friends littering the fields with no time to bury them all. Or was it the deafening roar of cannons, shells shrieking and bursting, and muskets rattling during horrific day-long battles? Or the cries of the wounded haunting their night-mares? Those who died quickly were lucky.

Cotton—and the slave labor used to grow it— had led the South to fight, and ultimately lose, this appalling and devastating war. In five years, over 620,000 men died and over a million were wounded. It was a staggering price to pay, but at the war's end, slavery was finally abolished. Many black workers, given their freedom, chose to move north, fearful of the lingering hatred of pro-slavery groups. And surprisingly, though the plantation owners had always protested that slavery was crucial to their high levels of cotton production, within seven years the South was able to produce as much cotton as it had before the war started.

Today cotton is grown mainly in China, India, the United States, Pakistan, Brazil, and Turkey. The United States is the top exporter of cotton yarn and fabric.

6

CACAO

PROS + CONS

Cacao is the main ingredient in chocolate, and chocolate gives you energy. It also puts you in a relaxed and happy mood by awakening a hormone in your brain called serotonin. Plus, chocolate has antioxidants that can help you to stay healthy. So go ahead, eat chocolate (dark chocolate, high in cacao, has the most health benefits). But beware . . . it can be hard to stop. While researchers say there's no such thing as an actual addiction to chocolate, many people do crave its sweetness, smooth texture, and tempting smell. And your mother is right: eating it before a meal will spoil your appetite.

BORN
In South America's Amazon rainforest.

AGE
Probably at least 3,000 years old.

DISLIKES
Too much sun, and crowding. When trees are crowded they are vulnerable to diseases and to insects like mealybugs, which spread a deadly plant virus.

LIKES
Constant warmth, with humidity and shade, and prefers lower elevations. These conditions are only found in places close to the equator: Malaysia, central Africa, the Caribbean, and the northern half of South America.

STATS
Cacao beans grow on an evergreen tree, in football-shaped seed pods, when the tree is three to four years old. Each pod carries 30 to 40 whitish, almond-shaped seeds, called beans.

PENNSYLVANIA [2013]

Kailyn loves chocolate, and one of her favorite books is Charlie and the Chocolate Factory, *by Roald Dahl. She loves the part where "Charlie put the mug to his lips, and as the rich warm creamy chocolate ran down his throat into his empty tummy, his whole body from head to toe began to tingle with pleasure, and a feeling of intense happiness spread over him." That's just how chocolate makes her feel, too!*

So Kailyn has always wanted to visit a real chocolate factory, to see how small, hard cacao beans are turned into sweet, smooth, delicious chocolate.

Today Kailyn is getting her wish. On her tour of the chocolate factory she sees how the beans are roasted at a set temperature for an exact amount of time. Then the shells are cracked to get at the "nibs" inside. Apparently, these little bits hold the secret to chocolate's taste. The next step is to grind the nibs into a product called "liquor" (even though it has nothing to do with alcohol). Then the liquor is squeezed to remove the fat called cacao butter, and what's left is "cake." When it's ground up, it's cocoa powder, which is what her mom uses to make brownies.

The best part of the tour is the rich, chocolaty aroma. Kailyn can smell the different flavors mixed with the "liquor" and sugar to make chocolate for eating. Then it goes through one more process, called conching, where it's smoothed to blend the flavors and improve the texture. Now the chocolate is just about ready to pour into molds for candies of various kinds. Kailyn really hopes there will be samples!

PLANT FACT

Chocolate will keep forever in the freezer. But can you resist eating it for that long?

The Story of Cacao

CHOCOLATE IS A UNIQUE SWEET TREAT, one of the world's favorite flavors. But have you ever given any thought to where it comes from?

Chocolate, in its original form as cacao beans, started out in Central America, was carried across the ocean to make new fans in Europe, and eventually was shipped back to chocolate lovers in North America. Incredibly, many children in the countries where cacao is grown today have never even tasted chocolate.

WE'LL NEVER GROW TIRED OF CHOCOLATE

Cacao is mainly grown in about 20 developing countries, but it is mostly enjoyed in more prosperous industrialized countries, where a few large companies process and manufacture different chocolate products. Each year, farmers worldwide grow around 3.5 million tons of cacao beans—that's the weight of about 80 battleships.

Today, powdered cocoa flavors baked treats, hot chocolate, chocolate milk, and chocolate ice cream, and makes chocolate coatings for candy. There's also "white chocolate," which is made with cacao butter (the oil from the cacao bean) but no powder. And cacao butter has other surprising uses. Because of its smooth texture, it is found in soaps, cosmetics, and lotions.

Chocolate Money?

Wʜᴇɴ ᴛʜᴇ Sᴘᴀɴɪsʜ ᴇxᴘʟᴏʀᴇʀ Hᴇʀɴᴀɴᴅᴏ Cᴏʀᴛᴇ́s traveled to Central America in 1519, he was introduced to chocolate —the Aztec emperor Montezuma II famously drank 50 cups of chocolate a day!—and he soon realized that cacao beans were more precious than gold. In fact, the native Mayans and Aztecs used the cacao beans as money, and used gold only for decorations.

Cortés overran the Aztecs, and soon afterward, seeing an opportunity to get rich, he set up many cacao plantations. But where were the workers who would grow the cacao? Well, hundreds of thousands of African slaves who had been brought to Caribbean islands to work on sugar plantations ended up growing cacao instead, to fill the labor shortage.

WILL THAT BE *CHOCOLATL*, OR COCOA?

The Olmecs of Mexico were the first to make a drink from cacao beans. And the Aztecs had their own way of preparing the beans to make their bitter *chocolatl* drink. They believed the god Quetzalcoatl had sent this "food of the gods" to give them wisdom and power. To make *chocolatl*, ground cacao beans were moistened with water and mixed with spicy chili peppers. After the drink was poured back and forth from one container to another, it made a frothy, spicy treat.

Three centuries later, in 1828, a Dutchman, Coenraad Van Houten, invented a press to squeeze out most of cacao's fat content, leaving just enough to bring out the chocolaty flavor. Then he added compounds to the remaining powder—now called **cocoa**—to help it blend smoothly with water or milk. We make these delicious chocolate drinks the same way today—usually without chili peppers.

The Dark Side of Chocolate

In 1585, THE FIRST SHIPMENT OF CACAO BEANS reached Spain, and European taste buds would never be the same again. Cacao quickly became a much-desired trade item. Once people tasted cocoa powder and chocolate candy in Europe, there was more demand for the product than the plantations could handle. By the mid-1800s, the world was facing a cacao shortage.

To increase production, the Portuguese next set up new cacao plantations on the Atlantic islands of São Tomé and Príncipe, off the west coast of Africa. The climate was right and the cacao plants thrived. And when the plantations needed laborers—well, the islands were very close to the Portuguese colony of Angola. Angola had long been a key player in the slave trade and exported more than a million slave laborers to the Americas.

The big chocolate companies in England—Fry's, Cadbury, Rowntree's—bought their cacao beans from the Portuguese islands. England had outlawed slavery at home and in its own colonies in 1834, but reports were emerging about the abuse of slave workers on the plantations. Were they true? If English manufacturers

stopped buying from the Portuguese plantations, it would mean lost profits and lost jobs in the chocolate factories at home, a lost market for the growers who were completely dependent on cacao, and even more hardship for the workers, who would no longer be needed.

In the early 20th century, unable to find a satisfactory way to end the use of slavery, European cacao buyers stopped buying from the Portuguese islands, and established plantations of their own in their colonies in West Africa: Côte d'Ivoire, Nigeria, and the Gold Coast (now called Ghana). Even so, on some of the large plantations the practice of using slave labor continued.

Côte d'Ivoire, a French colony, became the largest single cacao producer when many Africans began to grow it on their own small farms. Its economy boomed during the mid-1900s, but when world cacao prices tumbled (due to factors such as weather conditions during growing season and consumer demand for cacao), Côte d'Ivoire's profits fell too. Cacao farmers knew they could save money by using low-cost labor from neighboring African countries.

THE GREAT CHOCOLATE INVENTORS

Coenraad Van Houten discovers how to make powdered cocoa.

Three brothers, **Joseph**, **Francis**, and **Richard Fry**, create the first solid chocolate made with cacao butter and sugar.

George and **Richard Cadbury** make the first boxed chocolates.

Daniel Peter and **Henri Nestlé** create Swiss milk chocolate using powdered milk.

Milton S. Hershey creates Hershey's Kisses.

A Sour Business

In the late 1990s, startling news came to the world's attention. Global organizations that monitor working conditions learned that as many as 15,000 children of poor families had been lured to Côte d'Ivoire with promises of good wages. In fact, reports showed young boys of 12 to 16 were sold to cacao growers, made to work in brutal conditions, and denied the freedom to go home. Some were rescued and told journalists how they'd been beaten, given little food, and made to swing heavy machetes to cut open cacao pods, or carry huge sacks of beans. They had to handle toxic pesticides with no protection. They were not paid for working 12-hour days, and they were kept locked in sheds at night in case they ran away. This news put European and American buyers in the shocking position of appearing to support abusive child labor if they continued to trade with Côte d'Ivoire. And people worried that buying chocolate meant they were supporting this inhuman treatment of African children.

Since 2001, groups in the United States have tried—so far unsuccessfully—to pass a law requiring the labeling of chocolate products to certify that they do not contain cacao from growers who continue to abuse young workers. And child labor remains a way of life in West African cacao-growing regions. But organizations are still working on behalf of children by encouraging chocolate makers to sell their products at "fair trade" prices. They can then guarantee cacao producers a greater share of the profits so they, in turn, can afford to pay young workers, improve their living and working conditions, and allow them to go to school.

7

CINCHONA

NAME

Named by Swedish botanist Linnaeus after the Spanish Countess of Chinchón. Pronounced *sin-kona*. Also known as Jesuits' bark, Peruvian bark, quinine bark, fever-bark tree.

PROS + CONS

Cinchona's claim to fame is that its bark contains high levels of quinine, used to treat malaria. The Countess of Chinchón is said to be the first European cured of that disease by the plant, in Peru in 1638. Recently, though, cinchona has made headlines for less positive reasons. After the cinchona tree was brought to the Galápagos Islands, and to the Hawaiian islands, it became invasive, which means it chokes out the regions' native plants. Scientists want to find ways to remove it before it crowds the native plants out of existence.

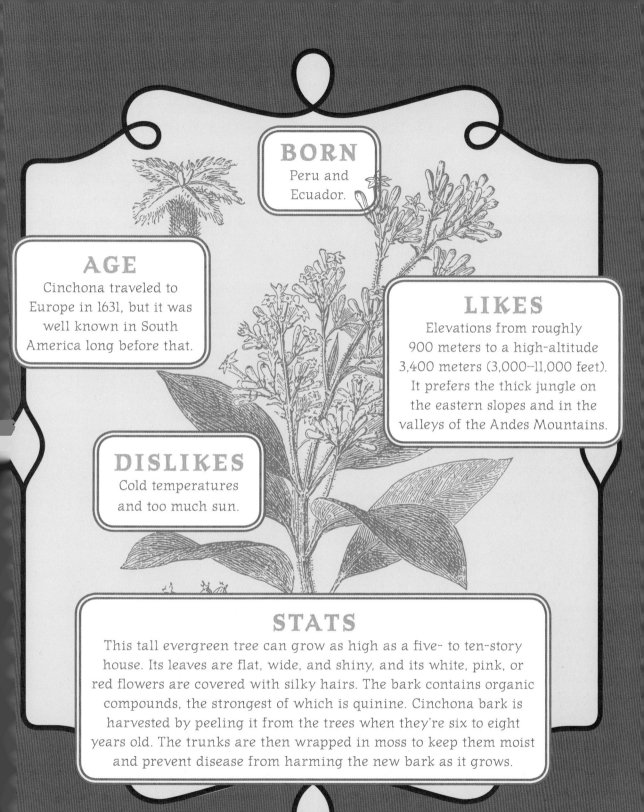

BORN
Peru and Ecuador.

AGE
Cinchona traveled to Europe in 1631, but it was well known in South America long before that.

LIKES
Elevations from roughly 900 meters to a high-altitude 3,400 meters (3,000–11,000 feet). It prefers the thick jungle on the eastern slopes and in the valleys of the Andes Mountains.

DISLIKES
Cold temperatures and too much sun.

STATS
This tall evergreen tree can grow as high as a five- to ten-story house. Its leaves are flat, wide, and shiny, and its white, pink, or red flowers are covered with silky hairs. The bark contains organic compounds, the strongest of which is quinine. Cinchona bark is harvested by peeling it from the trees when they're six to eight years old. The trunks are then wrapped in moss to keep them moist and prevent disease from harming the new bark as it grows.

ON THE MISSOURI RIVER
[1804]

At 18 years old, George is proud to be the youngest member of the Corps of Discovery led by Captains Meriwether Lewis and William Clark, setting off to explore the American West. He's been watching Captain Lewis write journal notes about the strange new plants and animals they've seen—like the incredibly fast pronghorn antelope, the curious barking prairie dogs, and immense herds of buffalo. Nothing to fear there. But he's heard terrifying stories from the natives they've encountered about giant, ferocious grizzly bears. He's not keen to meet one of those.

So far, the worst thing George has had to deal with is the millions of mosquitoes in the swamps along the Missouri River. The smelly paste of tallow and hog's lard they smear on their skin is supposed to deter them, but masses of the annoying bugs stick to it. Even the smoky fires fail to keep them from swarming around George's face while he's eating. Captain Lewis has told him to use netting over his bedroll to fend them off at night.

George will be glad to move out of these swampy areas, where the men have been getting sick. Acting as the expedition's doctor, Captain Lewis is treating their fevers with medicine made from tree bark. George only hopes he can stay well long enough to make it all the way to the Pacific Ocean . . . and home again.

PLANT FACT

The cinchona tree is shown in the coat of arms on Peru's flag.

The Story of Cinchona Bark

I<small>T'S ALMOST TOO UNBELIEV-ABLE TO BE TRUE</small>: the single cure for a disease first seen in Europe came from the bark of a tree that once grew only in South American jungles. But for centuries, mystery surrounded the cinchona tree and its ability to treat the often deadly illness called malaria (*mal aria* is Italian for "bad air").

People had long been aware of the power of cinchona bark to treat fevers. A monk in Peru was the first person to write about it, way back in the 1600s. In Europe, malaria was common, but no cure was known until Jesuit priests brought cinchona bark there in the 1640s. In Protestant countries, though, people were suspicious of the Catholic Jesuits, and just as distrustful of the malaria remedy they called "Jesuits' bark."

One problem with the remedy was that it didn't always work. At the time, no one realized that of the more than 40 species of cinchona being harvested in Peru and Ecuador, many had no effect on malaria at all. The medicinal value came from chewing the bark of the right tree species, or drinking water in which the bark had been soaked. But no one really understood the science behind cinchona until 1820, when French scientists found the reason for its effectiveness. Cinchona bark contains a chemical compound called quinine (from the native word *quina*, meaning bark). That's what gives it its fever-fighting properties.

HOW DOES MALARIA WORK?

Malaria is caused by a parasite that spends part of its life cycle in the anopheles mosquito. The insect injects its saliva—including the parasite—into human blood cells before sucking out blood. Once inside a human body, the parasite moves quickly to the liver. There it multiplies, then invades more red blood cells, destroying them. A person with malaria will have chills and fevers that return several times within a couple of weeks.

The disease can cause liver and spleen damage, and death. But not everyone who gets malaria will die from it. Some people are only carriers of the parasite—carriers transfer the disease if bitten by a malarial-type mosquito which then bites someone else.

Malaria occurs everywhere on Earth except Antarctica and a few isolated islands. Each year, 1.5 million people die of malaria, mostly in sub-Saharan Africa.

The Battle FOR the Bark

Throughout the 17th and 18th centuries, people were slowly accepting cinchona bark as a malaria remedy—after all, rumor had it that it was being used to treat the noblest members of the European royal courts. And Europeans badly wanted to establish colonies in some tropical regions where the disease was widespread. The solution seemed clear when the explorer David Livingstone found that high doses of the remedy worked to fight malaria during his travels in central Africa in the 1800s.

The race was on. The country that claimed the supply of cinchona in the Andes Mountains would get rich by controlling its trade. But finding and transporting cinchona was difficult in dense South American jungles, where there were no roads. Was there an easier way? What if cinchona trees could be grown in other tropical places?

Botanists began to search for and gather seedlings and seeds, with the idea of establishing new cinchona plantations in India and Indonesia. However, this idea didn't sit well with the Spanish, who controlled the sources of cinchona. They didn't want to lose their income from the bark. The other countries resorted to smuggling seedlings or seeds out of Peru and Ecuador.

Transporting the plant was not the only challenge, though. Cinchona is a finicky plant that didn't take well to growing outside of its Andean mountain home. As a result, it would be 30 years before the Dutch established a successful plantation of cinchona trees in Java, Indonesia, and the first bark was not ready to harvest until 1865.

WARDIAN CASES

When new plants were discovered in remote parts of the world, botanists needed an effective way to transport them back to their home countries. The Wardian case was invented in 1830 by Nathaniel B. Ward. It was a terrarium that enclosed a mini-ecosystem containing all the soil, water, and air a plant needed to live. Inside the sealed box with glass sides, plants gave off oxygen at night and carbon dioxide in the daytime. Water vaporized, condensed on the glass, and trickled back into the soil. Protected from disease, plants were able to withstand sea voyages of many months when carefully packed in Wardian cases.

GETTING CINCHONA OUT OF SOUTH AMERICA

French collectors' seedlings are lost at sea or stolen.

The Dutch smuggle seedlings and seeds to Java, but they turn out to be the wrong species— not effective against malaria.

The English smuggle seedlings to India. Some grow, but again they are the wrong species.

The English succeed in sending seeds to London, where interest has faded. The Dutch who buy them finally establish successful plantations in Java by 1890.

The world's cinchona supply comes mainly from South America, central Africa, and Indonesia.

Malaria Takes its Toll

Meanwhile, there was a growing shortage of quinine. To obtain it, cinchona trees in the jungles were being cut down or their bark entirely stripped. This killed them, of course, and few new trees were planted.

Soldiers in the American Civil War, from 1861–65, were among those who suffered greatly from the lack of quinine. To make matters worse, the connection between malaria and the mosquitoes that spread it would not be confirmed until almost 1900. Civil War soldiers slogged through hot, humid swamps, slept in the open in rain-soaked fields, dug trenches, and built roads—all activities that placed them near stagnant-water breeding grounds for mosquitoes. Over 1 million soldiers in the Union army alone caught malaria, and 10,000 died from it. After the Civil War, many soldiers returning home carried the malaria parasite in their blood, spreading the disease throughout the United States.

Quinine would also have made a significant difference when France began to build the Panama Canal, a deep-water link between the Atlantic and Pacific oceans, in 1881. Within three years, workers were dying from malaria at the rate of 100 a month. The French construction company had decided not to supply quinine to workers because of its high price. When the United States took over the project in 1903, they brought mosquito controls, and quinine.

During World War II, it looked as though American soldiers in the South Pacific and North Africa would have a secure supply of quinine to combat malaria. That is, until Japan occupied Indonesia and cut off access to its cinchona plantations. Thousands of American soldiers died of malaria. By the end of the war, though, a synthetic form of quinine was developed. Had the world's battle against malaria finally been won?

Still Fighting

INCREDIBLY, THE STORY IS NOT OVER. Even though the World Health Organization thought in the 1960s that malaria might be under control, it has made a comeback. It seems the malaria parasite has become resistant to synthetic quinine. Now the cinchona plantations in Java, mostly abandoned after World War II, are being restored, and seeds from those trees have been replanted in South America. Until a vaccine is developed, natural quinine from cinchona bark may remain the best control for a disease that affects 500 million people each year. In 2009, researchers discovered that chimpanzees in Africa were the original source of malaria. This knowledge could help them find a vaccine.

It is ironic that cinchona bark allowed Europeans—the explorers and conquerors who took malaria to new lands—to expand their empires with colonies in India and Africa, places malaria had kept them out of for centuries. What other miracle cures might exist in the rapidly shrinking rainforests of the world?

OTHER USES FOR CINCHONA

Quinine is only one of cinchona's useful ingredients. Another compound, quinidine, is a treatment for abnormal heart rhythm, muscle cramps, and headache. And quinine also flavors tonic water, a carbonated drink often mixed with alcohol. So why couldn't we just drink tonic water to relieve malaria? You'd need to down more than 600 glasses a day of modern tonic water for the amount of quinine to be effective.

8

RUBBER

NAME

In 1770, an English scientist, Joseph Priestly, discovered that small cubes of latex worked well to "rub out" pencil marks. He called the substance "rubber," and the name stuck.

PROS + CONS

Worldwide, a billion rubber tires wear out each year. If they all ended up in landfill, imagine what a pile that would make! Their shape traps air and methane gas, which tends to make them rise to the top, and stacks of stored tires have hollow spaces that hold water where mosquitoes can breed. If they catch fire, tires can burn for weeks, giving off toxic smoke and polluting water runoff from firefighting. On the positive side, tires can be recycled—at half the cost of making new rubber—which saves energy and raw materials and reduces pollution. Shredded into crumbs, recycled rubber is mixed with asphalt to pave roads, or used for mats and floor coverings in arenas and playgrounds—that way you get a bouncier landing when you fall.

BORN

Amazon rainforest, Brazil.

AGE

Rubber was already thousands of years old by the time European explorers saw the indigenous peoples of Central America using it, and that was in the 16th century.

DISLIKES

Frost. Also a fungus called South American leaf blight, which spreads quickly among trees planted too closely together.

LIKES

Plenty of rainfall and shade.

STATS

Natural rubber is made from latex, a white sap of the Brazilian rubber tree (*hevea brasiliensis*). The rubber tree can grow to the height of a 15-story building. Rubber trees reproduce when their beanlike pods ripen and explode to scatter the seeds. Trees can be tapped for 15 to 30 years.

MAYAN RIVIERA [2013]

Connor pores over the guidebook his parents bought to plan the family vacation to Mexico. He can't wait to hit the beaches, go snorkeling, and eat real tacos. The day trip to see the ancient Mayan ruins at Chichén Itzá might be the most exciting part, though. His friend Jake, who went there last year, told him about the spooky tunnel to a hidden temple and the gigantic mural of a battle scene.

But Connor is keen to see the Great Ball Court. It's supposed to be the biggest one ever discovered, with walls as tall as a four-story building. Ancient Mayans played a game that sounds kind of like soccer to Connor. He's finding it hard to believe that more than 3,000 years ago, people used balls shaped from raw rubber collected from rubber trees—and they could really bounce! The guidebook's description says it was solid rubber, and it could weigh more than a big, heavy watermelon. Man, that would hurt if it hit you! The players had to use their hips, legs, or arms—not hands or feet—to bounce the balls off the sloping court walls.

Even though the exact rules of the game aren't known, Jake told Connor that sometimes the leader of the losing team would be killed as a sacrifice to the Mayan gods, and then his skull might even be wrapped in rubber to make a new ball. It's a good thing his soccer team doesn't have to worry about that, Connor thinks, because he's the team captain!

PLANT FACT

People once used wax, pumice stone, and even lumps of bread to "rub out" pencil marks. Messy . . . and kind of hard on the paper. We can thank an Englishman, Edward Nairne, for making the first commercial rubber erasers in 1770.

The Story of Rubber

IT BOUNCES! IT STRETCHES! IT CUSHIONS! IT GRIPS! Rubber can be molded into so many shapes, it's no wonder it's found everywhere. Look around: it's the elastic in your clothing, the soles of your shoes, a hockey puck, party balloons, the tennis ball you play with, the rubber bands that hold things together, and, of course, tires of all kinds (tires use about three-quarters of the world's rubber production).

In Mexico, as far back as 1525, indigenous peoples used rubber for waterproof footwear, bottles, and balls for playing games. But when rubber was taken to Europe, people weren't interested in this strange stuff that got sticky in the heat and brittle in the cold. It took the discovery of a process called **vulcanization** to get the inventions rolling out, and the value of rubber suddenly bounced to great heights. How did a single plant—the rubber tree—set off both an economic boom and bust in an incredibly short time?

VULCANIZATION MAKES RUBBER WORK

The latex that tappers collect from rubber trees does not look or feel rubbery at all. Latex is a liquid that flows from shallow cuts in the bark of mature trees. It becomes rubber after it is pressed, to remove water, and then heated and molded into various shapes. But early versions of rubber became sticky in hot weather or brittle if it got too cold.

Then, in 1839, Charles Goodyear, an American hardware dealer, was experimenting by mixing latex with sulphur. He dropped some on a hot stove. The new leathery substance held its shape and nothing would dissolve it. Later called vulcanization, the process made rubber durable, yet flexible at any temperature, and vulcanized rubber soon began to fill a long list of industrial and household needs . . . and it made far better hockey pucks than wood! The first round rubber pucks were made in Montreal, in the 1880s.

Who Controls the Rubber?

In the late 19th century, England was eager to use its new factories to make money from natural resources found around the world. Unfortunately, rubber grew only in difficult-to-reach jungles in South America, and if something is hard to get, it costs a lot to produce it. But what if rubber tree plantations could be set up in England's colonies in Southeast Asia? Plantations there would be connected to important sea trade routes, and a huge workforce of Indian, Chinese, and Japanese laborers would be on hand to help England make rubber more easily and cheaply.

Only one big question remained: would rubber trees actually grow outside of the Brazilian jungle?

The answer: ship seeds to London's Kew Gardens. Researchers there would plant them and cultivate the rubber tree seedlings under controlled conditions. Sounds simple? It wasn't. The first seeds shipped to England spoiled during the long sea voyage. Another attempt resulted in only twelve seeds germinating. Six seedlings were sent to researchers in India, but they died too.

Clearly, the English researchers would have to get a lot more seeds, and hope enough of them survived the journey to try their experiment. Eventually, in 1876, the Englishman Henry Wickham collected 70,000 seeds . . . but by then he had to smuggle them out of Brazil. Why the secrecy? There was no law against exporting the seeds, since no one believed rubber trees would actually grow outside the country. But 10 years earlier, cinchona plants, valuable as a treatment for malaria, had been stolen, and Brazilian officials weren't keen on losing another important native plant. Wickham worried that inspectors might stall his shipment to demand permits. The rubber seeds might begin to spoil and be worthless. So, under cover of night, he loaded the ship and didn't list the seeds on the cargo manifest.

Wickham personally accompanied his precious goods back to Kew Gardens, taking great care of them at sea. Success! Although only 2,700 of the seeds germinated, it was enough to start the first plantations in Ceylon (now called Sri Lanka), Singapore, and Malaysia.

KEW GARDENS

The Royal Botanic Gardens at Kew, along the Thames River near London, England, was created in 1759 to gather and share knowledge about plants being discovered by global explorers. One of its important goals was growing these new plants throughout the expanding British Empire. The Royal Botanic Gardens supplied cinchona seeds to Indian colonies in 1867, and rubber seedlings to Southeast Asian colonies in 1876. If you go there today, you'll find the world's largest collection of plant life.

Henry Ford's Vision

In the 1930s, the car maker Henry Ford dreamed of creating an industrial wonderland beside a river in the Amazon jungle. His vision inspired him to buy 1 million hectares (2.5 million acres) of land to build a megacity and rubber production plant he would call Fordlândia. Along with the rubber tree plantation, Fordlândia would have housing for workers, shops, and a wharf big enough to handle oceangoing cargo ships. Ford was a man with a dream, and he ignored the advice of local people who knew that clear-cutting the rainforest to build Fordlândia would destroy the nutrient-rich soils that rubber trees needed. Without the canopy of trees essential to the water cycle and for shelter from the tropical sun, the bulldozed land would dry out. As well, planting trees closely in rows would make it easy for blight to spread. It's too bad Ford didn't listen.Less than 15 years later, after struggling unsuccessfully to battle nature, he abandoned Fordlândia, which is now almost a ghost town.

RUBBER SETS THE WORLD IN MOTION

Before rubber came along, horse-drawn carriages and other vehicles rolled along on wooden or metal wheels. The first rubber tires were a relief, but solid rubber still made for a bumpy, uncomfortable ride. Things went more smoothly when the pneumatic tire—a rubber tire filled with air—was invented in 1845.

Where the Rubber Hits the Road

By 1899, A MILLION TREES were supplying enough rubber to satisfy the hungry world market. Rubber production in Southeast Asia overtook Brazil's in 1913. Soon more and more cars were hitting the roads, and they all needed tires. But Brazil had lost its hold on the world's rubber market.

SYNTHETIC RUBBER

Because of the high demand for natural rubber, scientists began to experiment with ways to make synthetic, or artificial, rubber in the late 1800s. Their first success came in Germany around 1930, and just in time. New technologies were creating a demand that rubber plantations couldn't fill. For instance, rubber for tires and parts had allowed war machinery to keep moving during World War I. Then, in World War II, the Japanese occupied Malaysia, blocking the world's access to most rubber tree plantations.

Synthetic rubber did the job, and by 1964 it had taken over three-quarters of the world's rubber market. But it takes natural gas and oil to make synthetic rubber. A spike in oil prices in 1973 sent the costs so high that natural rubber rebounded to take back one-third of the market. Today, twice as much synthetic rubber is produced, but half of all automobile and aircraft tires use the harder and more durable natural rubber.

9

POTATO

NAME

From the Spanish *patata*. Also known as Irish potato, spud, pratie. Sweet potatoes and yams aren't really potatoes—they belong to a different plant family.

PROS + CONS

Potatoes contain every key nutrient except vitamin B12. They're good for you. So that means it's okay to eat lots of French fries and potato chips, right? Well, once in a while for a treat is okay. The potato itself is fine—the downside comes with the way we cook it. French fries are fried in oil, and chips are made with lots of salt. The high fat and sodium content can lead to obesity, among other health problems. So try them baked, mashed, or roasted instead (and hold the butter and sour cream).

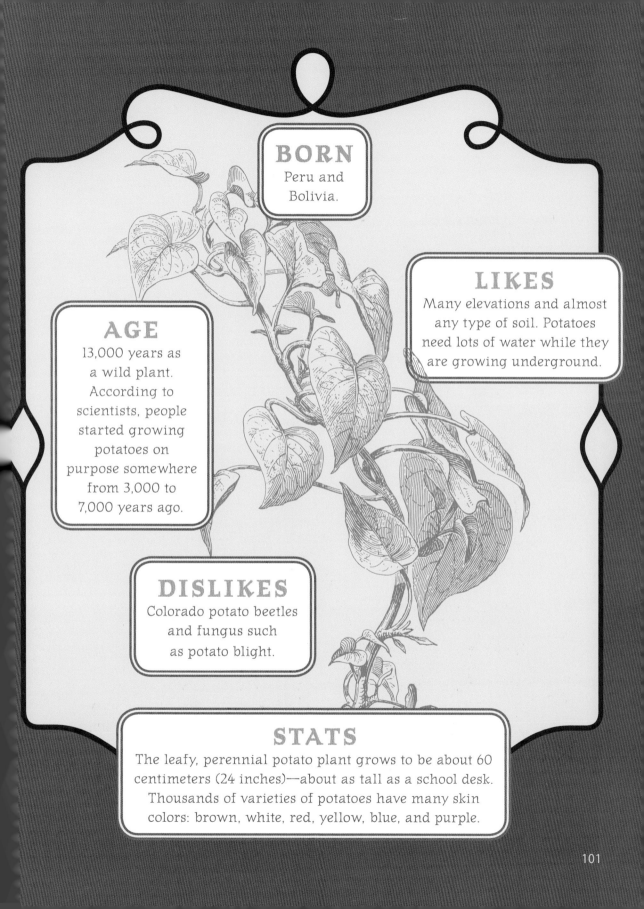

BORN
Peru and
Bolivia.

LIKES
Many elevations and almost
any type of soil. Potatoes
need lots of water while they
are growing underground.

AGE
13,000 years as
a wild plant.
According to
scientists, people
started growing
potatoes on
purpose somewhere
from 3,000 to
7,000 years ago.

DISLIKES
Colorado potato beetles
and fungus such
as potato blight.

STATS
The leafy, perennial potato plant grows to be about 60
centimeters (24 inches)—about as tall as a school desk.
Thousands of varieties of potatoes have many skin
colors: brown, white, red, yellow, blue, and purple.

PERU [2013]

Dominga is eager to go back to the fields this morning to see how the potatoes are doing. Yesterday, she and her parents began making chuño. This is a special way of preparing potatoes in the freezing temperatures of Peru's Altiplano, the high-altitude plains, where it has been done the same way for thousands of years. Dominga knows that chuño even fed the ancient peoples of the Andes. It was an easy food to make, and because the potatoes were basically freeze-dried they kept for years if permanently frozen and stored underground. She knows people even used chuño to pay their taxes.

The potatoes have been spread out in the open to freeze overnight. It freezes most nights this high up in the Andes Mountains. Wearing rubber boots, Dominga will stomp on the potatoes, which squeezes out the water and bursts the skins. Then the potatoes will be protected from the warm sun before being left to freeze overnight again.

For three or four more days, Dominga will help with the trampling process. Then the potatoes will be washed, refrozen once more, and stomped on again to remove the skins. After it has dried for up to a week, the chuño will be ready to sell to city restaurants that like to promote Peru's traditional foods. And best of all, Dominga will get some to eat at home. Then she might help her mother stuff the chuño with meat and cheese, or mix it with meat and vegetables for soups or stew. She even knows how to make dessert from chuño. But first, time for more stomping!

PLANT FACT

In 1995, potato plants were onboard for the launch of the space shuttle *Columbia* and traveled in its Microgravity Astroculture Laboratory. Scientists at NASA believe that growing plants onboard will be important for long-duration space flights, providing food and water to crews, as well as replenishing oxygen and helping to remove excess carbon dioxide from the air.

The Story of the Potato

THE BROWN LUMPY "SPUD" MAY NOT WIN PRIZES
for looks, but it sure tastes good. Lucky for us that it's also one
of the most nutritious foods the world has known. Today, it is the
world's fourth most important food crop.

The Spanish Conquistadors who came to Peru were looking for
gold, but they also found potatoes. In 1570 they brought this native
South American food back to Europe, where potatoes slowly won
fans because they were so easy to grow on a small amount of land.
Potatoes could even be planted in fields that were not producing other
crops because they were lying fallow (given a rest from grain crops).
They were a cheaper food than bread, and quicker to prepare, too.

When the potato made its way to Ireland, it fed the people so well
that Ireland's population doubled between 1780 and 1841, to 8 million.
Even the poorly paid farmers who herded cattle for wealthy English
landowners could grow enough potatoes on their small, rented plots
of land to feed their large families. Cooked with milk, their potato
meals were plain and simple, but nourishing.

UNPOPULAR POTATOES

Gardeners in Europe didn't take eagerly to potatoes in the 1600s. They thought the plants were poisonous (some plants in the same plant family, nightshade, really are toxic). Some people thought potatoes might cause diseases—the lumpy spuds reminded them of the disfiguring effects of leprosy. In Russia, potatoes were called "devil's apples," and in 1840, government orders that peasants must plant this nutritious food led to several years of "potato riots." The French disliked the way potato starch used in baking made their bread soggy. Many people thought potatoes were only fit for animal feed. Lucky animals!

People began to change their minds after Frederick the Great of Prussia came up with a clever trick. He posted guards on his potato garden at night. Were these odd plants so valuable? Peasants figured they must be, so they stole some to grow their own.

Potato Tragedy

Aʟʟ ᴏᴠᴇʀ Eᴜʀᴏᴘᴇ ɪɴ ᴛʜᴇ 1800s, growing populations needed to be fed. So Ireland's landowners started planting grain and hired more workers. But when grain prices fell, the land-owners saw more profit in switching over to raising cattle again. To do that, they needed to take back the valuable land they had rented out to all those Irish peasants. And they didn't need as many workers now, either. Soon, over 3 million people were out of work. But the peasants refused to move. How would they get by without at least a bit of land to grow potatoes? Little did they know the scale of the disaster that loomed ahead.

Far across the ocean, in Mexico, a fungus was attacking potato plants. It somehow made its way to the northeastern United States, and then it traveled to Europe on infected potatoes. The potato fungus first hit Ireland in 1845, with little warning. A patch of potatoes that was healthy in the evening would be black with rot the next morning. The "potato blight" completely wiped out the only food source for most poor Irish workers. Over a million starved or died from diseases in the extremely harsh winter of 1846, because they had sold everything, including most of their warm clothing, to buy food.

Worse still, the blight returned in 1847. The government would not give anyone aid, or allow them to live on charity in a workhouse until they gave up their land. But if the starving peasants left their homes, the landlords would burn them so no one could return.

POTATO BLIGHT

The blight that attacked Ireland's potatoes showed up near the end of the growing season, so it was called the "late blight." At first, farmers believed they had a promising crop. Then dark spots appeared, and later a fuzzy growth formed on the leaves and stems. The plants quickly decayed and died. As soon as the fungus appeared on the leaves, farmers frantically dug up the potatoes, thinking they'd be safe in storage, but they rotted within days. And the fungus had infected the soil, so new potatoes could not be planted. Three years of blight destroyed most potato crops throughout Europe. Until the late 1800s, no one knew the fungus could be controlled with a simple copper sulfate solution.

Potato Feast Becomes Famine

Soon a ragged parade of homeless people filled the
roads, heading to the cities, where they would beg for food or jobs.
Hunger and misery forced people to steal from each other. Those who
didn't die on the journey lined up outside workhouses, where a single
daily meal of oatmeal and water promised to keep them alive.

The famine years cut Ireland's population of 8 million in half.
Any people who could scrape together the price of sea passage left
their beloved country. Almost one and a half million people emigrated
out of Ireland to North America and Australia in the mid-1800s. No
one had been able to foresee that depending so completely on the potato
crop would result in one of the greatest human tragedies in history—
so many deaths, and a huge movement of people out of the country.
In America, though, it was the beginning of a flourishing Irish culture.

The potato is still grown in Ireland and has remained very popular,
but the ghost of famine still haunts people's memories. Today, one third
of the world's potatoes are grown in China and India.

POTATO MYTHS

Are you superstitious about black cats, walking under ladders, or Friday the 13th? What about potatoes? Some folks believe that if you rub a wart with a cut potato, then bury the potato in the ground, your wart will disappear as the potato rots. Others say a potato in your pocket can cure ailments like rheumatism. It's even said that one of the best parts of a potato is the skin, so be sure to eat it. Hey . . . that last one is not just a superstition! It's true: the skin has the most fiber, something our digestive system needs.

10

CORN

NAME

Maize, from the Spanish *maíz*.
Also known as "gift of the gods."

PROS + CONS

Corn is an incredibly important part of the diet of people all over the world—which means that growing it is big business, too. Scientists have studied corn's DNA in order to create better varieties of corn, so farmers can grow more of it on less land, with less expense. One type won't be damaged by most weed-killing chemicals, so the farmer can use those chemicals to wipe out all the weeds but leave the corn growing. Another is able to fight off insects like the European corn borer, which tunnels into ears and stalks. Today, over three-quarters of corn grown in the United States is genetically modified (GM) in some way. Is there a downside? Well, some people think changing a familiar plant in what seem like drastic ways might not be safe for human health. They think GM crops need much more study before being so widely used.

BORN
Mexico.

AGE
Imagine: corn might be 10,000 years old. Or even older—corn pollen found in Mexico suggests that wild corn species might have existed up to 80,000 years ago.

LIKES
Many different climates and elevations from sea level up to 3,658 meters (12,000 feet). Plenty of water and fertilizer. Corn likes light, but it likes darkness, too. Scientists have discovered proteins in corn that help the plant turn the starch it makes during the day into food for faster growth at night.

DISLIKES
Worms, beetles, and grasshoppers, which burrow into its ears or eat its leaves.

STATS
Ears of corn grow wrapped in the long, narrow leaves of the corn plant, and each one might contain 200 to 400 kernels. Cornstalks are thick and can grow as high as a third-story window, but most have been bred to reach just 2.5 meters (8.2 feet)—a little shorter than a basketball net—for easier picking.

BRITISH COLUMBIA [2013]

Hannah grabs her hat and races out to the barn. Uncle Brad is waiting for her to help mow a path through the cornfield for this year's corn maze. In May, her uncle planted a specially chosen seed that he knew would grow good, strong stalks. And the variety he chose would quickly grow high—high enough that even adults couldn't see over the top. But that's the beauty of being able to choose what type of corn to grow, her uncle told her. You know exactly what you're going to get. Hannah knows it's also important to plant just the right amount of corn. If the maze is too thin, you'll be able to see right through it. After all, getting lost in the maze is the whole point!

The maze will be around until Halloween. Then the corn this field produces will be used for cattle feed. Uncle Brad grows other types to sell in the farm market as corn on the cob. That corn will be ready for people to buy in late summer.

Hannah can hear the tractor engine rumbling behind the barn. It's her first year to drive it, and she's anxious to show her uncle that she can follow the GPS map to get the design of the maze just right. This year, the maze theme will be a trek through the solar system, with stops at planets and asteroids. Cool! Hannah plans to get her friends to try the maze with her after dark one evening, with flashlights. And she'll take along the cell phone, just in case they get lost!

PLANT FACT

Corn comes in many colors: the kernels might be yellow, white, blue, purple, black, or multicolored, like a type of maize called Indian corn. It also comes in hundreds of varieties, including popcorn, sweet corn (for corn on the cob), and flour corn (which is easy to grind and used for baking).

The Story of Corn

ARE YOU TALL LIKE YOUR PARENTS, or do you have your grandmother's red hair? Well, most of the plants described in this book still resemble their earliest ancestors. Corn is different.

Scientists have studied the genes of the modern corn plant, and they know it started life thousands of years ago as a tall wild grass called teosinte, which grew in Mexico. Teosinte didn't look like today's corn at all. It had small ears with maybe only a dozen kernels each. Those seeds could easily be scattered by birds and animals. Today's corn cannot seed itself like that—it has to be planted by humans. And that is the key to corn's amazing success. After centuries of changes brought about by farmers planting the varieties that people liked most, corn became first a nutritious food, and then the source of thousands of new products. How did a plant with such simple beginnings change the world in so many ways?

A Crop for Everyone, Everywhere

EVIDENCE TELLS US THAT CORN WAS FIRST CULTIVATED between 6,000 and 10,000 years ago. Mayans, Aztecs, and Incas used it every day. Those indigenous peoples had long practiced the science of selective plant breeding, even if they didn't call it that. Naturally, they chose the best corn from each season's crop and saved its seed to plant the next spring. It might have been the one that grew with less water, or ripened even in a shorter growing season, depending on what they needed most.

After Europeans arrived in the Americas, Native Americans taught them how to grow corn. The Spanish and Portuguese took it home with them in the 15th and 16th centuries. In the next century it spread to China, Indonesia, and Africa, where it was once traded for slaves. It's still a main part of the daily diet in many African countries.

"SISTER" CORN

Native Americans often planted corn along with beans and squash. The crops, known as the "three sisters," supported each other as they grew, and together provided all the nutrients of a healthy diet. Even corn husks had practical uses—they could be woven into mats or baskets, or made into corn-husk dolls. The leftover cobs could be burned as fuel, or hung from sticks as ceremonial rattles.

Corn Technology

IN THE 1800s, AMERICAN PIONEERS PLANTED CORN as they settled the western frontier. They, too, carefully chose which seeds to plant, to suit soil and climate conditions. They tilled the soil with wooden ploughs pulled by farm animals, then planted and harvested the corn by hand.

When new technologies, like the invention of tractors, made the work easier and faster, the farming business grew—and so did research into improving the quality and quantity of corn. In fact, corn has probably been studied more than any other plant.

In the early 1900s, researchers crossed different varieties of corn pollen to create new types of corn, called hybrids. But farmers had to be convinced that buying and planting this more expensive hybrid seed would bring better results than the less-efficient, but tried-and-true natural method of saving seed from their own crops. As it turned out, hybrid corn produced high yields even in the drought conditions of the Great Depression in the 1930s. It won fans just as the demand for food rose during World War II, and again after the war as worldwide populations grew. Today, of the 700 million tons of corn grown, most is hybrid. The United States supplies three-quarters of the world's corn, with China in second place.

CORN NEEDS US

Why can't corn seed itself, as so many other plants do? Take a close look at an ear of corn. You'll see hundreds of kernels so tightly packed together, and wrapped so securely in layers of leaves, that the wind cannot release them and rain cannot wash them individually to the ground. Birds or animals destroy the kernels by eating them. And if a cob just falls to the ground, the kernels do not drop off. They remain too close together for any to sprout and grow well. So just as we need corn, it depends on us. If humans stopped planting corn, it would become extinct.

The Gift of Corn

For many Native Americans, corn was their sacred mother. The Mayans worshipped corn as a gift from the gods. They believed that humans were made of corn, and they used it in ceremonies when a child was born. Corn planted in the child's name would be fed to the child until he was grown. Others believed corn had power to give protection if it was placed beside a child who was left alone.

To this day, Guatemalans fire a large cob of corn into the air with a rocket, believing the next harvest will be good if the corn flies high. Farmers in Belize feel that the positive spirit of corn is most present in the last ears that are picked. These seeds are mixed with blood from a chicken and planted in the next season, so the spirit will remain.

sneaky corn

Besides being a commonly eaten vegetable—North Americans eat on average about 4 kilograms (9 pounds) of fresh sweet corn per person per year—corn in other forms can be found in up to three-quarters of all grocery items. Corn is in meat (because animals are fed corn) and candy (when it's made with corn syrup). It gets into soap (which is made with corn oil) and toothpaste (which uses cornstarch for texture). Believe it or not, it's a filler in paint, and it even finds its way into car parts. And it might be in your lunch bag, even if it's not part of your meal, because corn is used to make some kinds of plastic containers. Corn-based plastic is biodegradable because the starch and sugar base means it can be composted.

Be a Corn Detective!

Among the thousands of products in a grocery store, could you tell which ones contain corn? Even if you read the labels, you won't always spot it. That's because it isn't usually called "corn." Manufacturers use a number of different names for cornstarch, corn syrup, or corn oil. Even ingredients like dextrose, lecithin, and sorbitol might actually come from corn.

Cornstarch is a fine powder made by grinding the corn kernel, called the endosperm. If a sauce, soup, or pudding needs thickening, cornstarch will do the job. It will also tenderize baking. When a cookie crumbles and melts in your mouth, that might be cornstarch at work. But it has a different effect on paper: in small amounts, cornstarch gives tissue paper its strength, while larger amounts make paper used for printing stiff, with a smooth surface.

Corn syrup comes from blending cornstarch with water and a protein that turns the mixture into a thick, sugary liquid. Besides sweetening things, corn syrup will help keep them fresh by holding moisture. Those marshmallows you use to make s'mores stay soft in the bag, and the graham crackers stay fresh a long time, because of corn syrup. It keeps your ice cream smooth, preventing sugary crystals from forming. And it's corn syrup that ensures chewing gum will stay soft—even when all the flavor has gone.

Corn oil—sold in bottles or as margarine—comes from squeezing the germ (the hard core) of the kernel under very high pressure. Almost half of the germ is oil, so it is available in large quantities. Corn oil doesn't change color when it's heated, which makes it a favorite product for frying. It won't change the flavor of the food, so you'll have to be a clever detective to know it's there.

A Food...and a Fuel?

NOT ALL CORN IS DESTINED TO BECOME FOOD for people or animals. Thousands of corn-based products have been created using modern technology. By the end of the 20th century, concerns about dwindling supplies of oil in the world led to the development of ethanol, an alternative fuel. This "biofuel" can be made from corn and blended in small amounts with gasoline. The United States produced 50 billion liters (13.2 billion gallons) of ethanol for transportation fuel in 2010. Using ethanol would seem to be a good way to use less oil and create less pollution. But studies show that corn-based ethanol isn't as efficient as we might hope. It takes so much energy to grow the corn—including the energy to run the farm machinery and make the fertilizer—and then convert the corn to fuel that the energy savings from using ethanol aren't as high as expected. And corn's importance in creating ethanol has driven up the price of this plant, causing huge problems and far-ranging consequences for many who depend on it as a food staple and livestock feed. Clearly there is still more to learn about corn.

SWEET? OR SOUR!

Many of your favorite processed foods, including sodas and fruit drinks, contain high-fructose corn syrup (HFCS), a sweetener made from cornstarch. It was developed in the 1970s, when it was cheaper to produce than cane or beet sugar (sucrose). But since 1990, studies have linked HFCS with a dramatic increase in obesity. They've found fructose doesn't satisfy the appetite as well as sucrose does, so we tend to eat more of foods containing it. As well, the liver changes fructose to a type of fat that is bad for the heart. So before you enjoy too many sweet foods, you might want to check the labels to see how much HFCS they contain.

Conclusion

THE YEARS FROM 1400 TO 1900 saw extraordinary changes for humankind. Plant discoveries drove much exploration and economic growth, bringing new knowledge while also contributing to a rapidly growing world population. By the end of the 1700s, Europeans had visited and claimed more than half of the world's lands. Scientists—among them doctors and botanists—studied and experimented with plants collected from around the globe. They established some 1,600 botanic gardens for this work at universities in Europe. It is work that continues to this day.

The world's population keeps growing. So we've cleared vast stretches of natural vegetation to make more room to grow food crops. The most dramatic example might be the tropical rainforest, a rich storehouse of biodiversity that continues to be cut and burned, and replaced by crops and livestock. Scientists are alarmed at the rate of this destruction, and the possibility of losing thousands of plants that could have important medicinal or nutritional uses before they've even been discovered. That's why there's a new urgency to **bioprospecting**—searching for plant products that might enrich our lives. Who knows what might still be out there waiting, with its roots in the ground and its leaves reaching to the sun?

ETHNOBOTANY IS THE SCIENTIFIC STUDY OF HOW PEOPLE, PLANTS, AND ENVIRONMENTS WORK TOGETHER.

Throughout the world, about half of all plant species are useful to people as food, medicine, or building materials, and in many other ways.

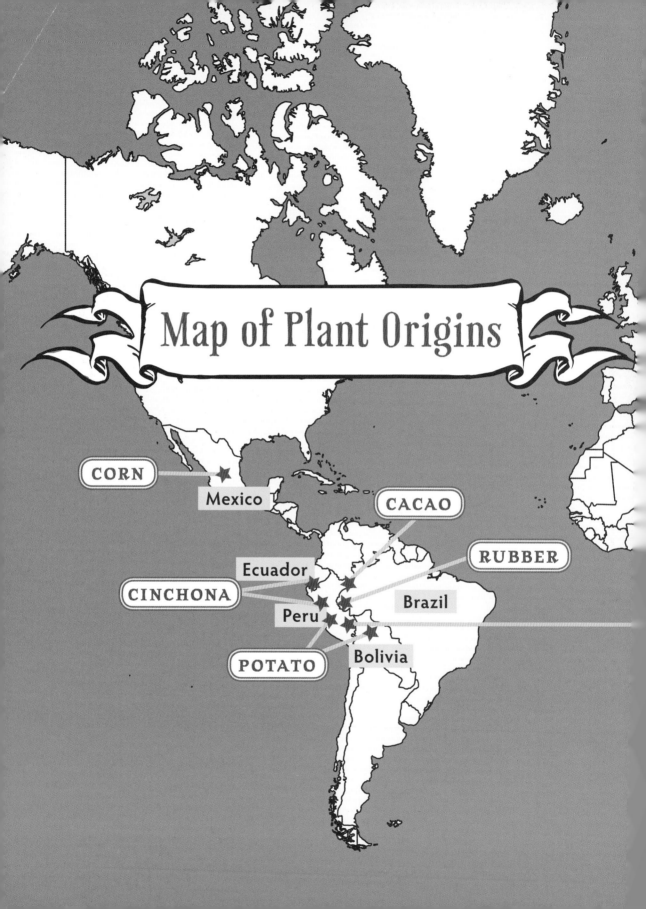

Map of Plant Origins

CORN
Mexico

CACAO

RUBBER

Ecuador

CINCHONA

Brazil

Peru

POTATO

Bolivia

PAPYRUS

TEA

Egypt

India

China

PEPPER

SUGARCANE

COTTON

Indonesia

New Guinea

SELECTED BIBLIOGRAPHY

Abbott, Elizabeth. *Sugar: A Bittersweet History*. Toronto: Penguin, 2008.

The Applied History Research Group. "The Sugar and Slave Trades." The European Voyages of Exploration, The University of Calgary, 1997. http://www.ucalgary.ca/applied_history/tutor/eurvoya/Trade.html

Baumgartner, Henry. "New light on Ancient Scrolls." *Mechanical Engineering*, April 2002, Vol. 124, Issue 4, p 80.

Board of Trustees of the Royal Botanic Gardens, Kew. "Black Pepper—History." Plant Culture: Exploring Plants and People. http://www.kew.org/plant-cultures/plants/black_pepper_history.html

Burba, Juliet. "Cinchona Bark." James Ford Bell Library. http://www.lib.umn.edu/bell/tradeproducts/cinchonabark

Cadbury, Deborah. *Chocolate Wars*. Toronto: Douglas & McIntyre, 2010.

Chanthavong, Samlanchith. "Chocolate and Slavery: Child Labor in Cote d'Ivoire." TED Case Studies. http://www1.american.edu/ted/chocolate-slave.htm

Doebley, J. F. "What is teosinte?" Doebley Lab. http://teosinte.wisc.edu/questions.html#what_is_teosinte

Elliott, William (Billy) A. "Civil War Letters of William (Billy) A. Elliott." Letters About the Civil War. http://www.civilwarhome.com/elliottletters.htm

Fussell, Betty Harper. *The Story of Corn*. New York: Alfred A. Knopf, 1992.

Gibson, Lance, and Garren Benson. "Origin, History, and Uses of Corn (Zea Mays)." Iowa State University Department of Agronomy, January 2002. http://www.agron.iastate.edu/courses/agron212/readings/corn_history.htm

Harrison, Absolom A. "Civil War Letter #1." Letters About the Civil War. http://www.civilwarhome.com/letter1.htm

Hobhouse, Henry. *Seeds of Change*. London: Papermac, 1999.

Interpreting Ancient Manuscripts Web. "Papyrus (5th Century BCE—8th Century CE)." http://legacy.earlham.edu/~seidti/iam/papyrus.html

Jackson, Joe. *The Thief at the End of the World: Rubber, Power and the Seeds of Empire*. New York: Penguin, 2008.

Macfarlane, Alan, and Iris Macfarlane. *The Empire of Tea*. New York: Overlook Press, 2004.

Morgan, Keith E. "The Rubber Tree (Hevea brasiliensis)." Southern Illinois University Carbondale/Ethnobotanical leaflets, 1999. http://www.ethnoleaflets.com//leaflets/rubber.htm

Musgrave, Toby, and Will Musgrave. *An Empire of Plants: People and Plants That Changed the World*. New York: Sterling, 2000.

Off, Carol. *Bitter Chocolate*. Toronto: Random House, 2006.

Reader, John. *Propitious Esculent: The Potato in World History*. London: Random House, 2008.

Rocco, Fiammetta. *The Miraculous Fever-Tree*. New York: HarperCollins, 2003.

Rose, Sarah. *For All the Tea in China: How England Stole the World's Favorite Drink and Changed History*. New York: Viking, 2010.

Shah, Sonia. *The Fever: How Malaria Has Ruled Humankind for 500,000 Years.* New York: Farrar, Straus & Giroux, 2010.

Slavery in America: "History. King Cotton: The Fiber of Slavery." http://www .slaveryinamerica.org/history/hs_es_cotton.htm

Turner, Jack. *Spice: The History of a Temptation.* New York: Alfred A. Knopf, 2004.

U.S. National Park Service. "African Americans in Slavery." http://www.nps.gov/ history/delta/underground/slave.htm

West, Jean M. "Sugar and Slavery: Molasses to Rum to Slaves." Slavery in America. http://www.slaveryinamerica.org/history/hs_es_sugar.htm

Yafa, Stephen. *Big Cotton: How a Humble Fiber Created Fortunes, Wrecked Civilizations, and Put America on the Map.* New York: Penguin, 2005.

Zuckerman, Larry. *The Potato: How the Humble Spud Rescued the Western World.* Winchester, MA: Faber & Faber, 1998.

FURTHER READING

Aronson, Marc. *Sugar Changed the World: A Story of Magic, Spice, Slavery, Freedom and Science.* Clarion, 2010.

Bailey, Katharine. *Vasco da Gama: Quest for the Spice Trade.* Crabtree, 2007.

Bartolleti, Susan Campbell. *Black Potatoes: Story of the Great Irish Famine 1845–1850.* Sandpiper, 2005.

Brocker, Susan. *Shockwave: Paper Trail: History of an Everyday Material.* Children's Press, 2007.

Burleigh, Robert. *Chocolate: Riches from the Rainforest.* Abrams, 2002.

Eagen, Rachel. *Biography of Sugar.* Crabtree, 2005.

Gondosch, Linda. *How Did Tea and Taxes Spark a Revolution?: And Other Questions About the Boston Tea Party.* Lerner, 2010.

Hopkinson, Deborah. *Up Before Daybreak: Cotton and People in America.* Scholastic, 2006.

Johnson, Sylvia. *Tomatoes, Potatoes, Corn and Beans: How the Food of the Americas Changed Eating Around the World.* Atheneum, 1997.

Kroll, Steven. *The Boston Tea Party.* Capstone, 2006.

Masters, Nancy. *The Cotton Gin (Inventions That Shaped the World).* Children's Press, 2006.

Morganelli, Adrianna. *The Biography of Chocolate.* Crabtree, 2005.

Ollhoff, Jim. *Malaria.* ABDO & Daughters, 2009.

Wells, Don. *The Spice Trade.* Weigl, 2005.

index

ACKNOWLEDGMENTS

I would like to acknowledge Ellen Borker and Jack Kaplan, volunteers at Brooklyn Botanic Garden, for planting the seeds of this book. Their research resulted in the sidebar "Ten Plants That Shook the World," published as part of a *Garden Design Magazine* article (November 1997).

I'm grateful to Annick Press for inviting me to take on this project. It was a pleasure to work with Catherine Marjoribanks, and once again with the Annick team.

My recognition and appreciation for this bountiful harvest of stories goes to: early explorers for their sense of adventure and courage; scientists and inventors for their imagination and curiosity; and ordinary people for their great personal sacrifices throughout history.

PHOTO CREDITS

ABOUT THE AUTHOR

Photo credit Jennifer Nicholson

Gillian Richardson has worked as a teacher-librarian in several Canadian provinces, and could never stop reading the books in her libraries. Then it became too hard to resist writing her own books. Now living near Shuswap Lake in British Columbia, she works at home as both a writer and a teacher of writing. She still loves reading (especially with a cup of tea close at hand), nature study, travel, and gardening. In her garden you will always find plants that attract birds, as well as corn and potatoes growing in the backyard vegetable patch.

Her previous book with Annick Press, *Kaboom! Explosions of All Kinds,* was honored with readers' choice award nominations, and won the 2010 Science Writing Award from the American Institute of Physics.

ABOUT THE ILLUSTRATOR

Photo credit Cara Taylor

Kim Rosen grew up in a suburb of Philadelphia and could usually be found in her room quietly drawing pictures. After high school, Kim moved to New York City and worked as an advertising designer for several years before realizing she was meant to be an Illustrator. Today, Kim can usually be found in her studio, quietly drawing pictures for clients all over the world.

Kim's illustrations are inspired by the life around her—the flowers in her garden, the vintage fabrics in her home, the painted architecture of New England, and the gestures and expressions of people in everyday situations. Her illustrations have appeared in magazines and newspapers including *The New Yorker, The Atlantic,* and *The Wall Street Journal.* She has also done illustration work for companies including Starbucks, Billabong, and American Express. Kim lives with her partner in Northampton, Mass., in their 115-year-old house.

IF YOU LIKED 10 PLANTS THAT SHOOK THE WORLD, CHECK OUT THESE BOOKS FROM ANNICK PRESS:

ANIMALS THAT CHANGED THE WORLD
by Keltie Thomas [paperback $12.95 hardcover $21.95]

"There's no question it will appeal to fact-loving middle graders..."
—*Kirkus Reviews*

"...is sure to be a hit with children, parents, teachers and librarians with its thought-provoking questions and answers. Highly recommended."
—*CM Magazine*

KABOOM! EXPLOSIONS OF ALL KINDS
by Gillian Richardson [paperback $12.95 hardcover $22.95]

"...an engrossing attention-getter, effectively tapping the sensationalism of all types of blasts." —*School Library Journal*

"...deserves to be read for general interest as well as educative purposes; it is truly a blast." —*Resource Links*

SPIKED SCORPIONS AND WALKING WHALES
by Claire Eamer [paperback $9.95 hardcover $19.95]

"Young scientists and naturalists will find this volume fascinating."
—*Resource Links*

"Highly entertaining, engaging and educational...an absolute must-read."
—*CM Magazine*